Hit by Pitch

Hit by Pitch

Ray Chapman, Carl Mays and the Fatal Fastball

Molly Lawless

McFarland & Company, Inc., Publishers
Jefferson, North Carolina, and London

Library of Congress Cataloguing-in-Publication Data

Lawless, Molly.
Hit by pitch : Ray Chapman, Carl Mays
and the fatal fastball / Molly Lawless.
p. cm.
Includes bibliographical references.

ISBN 978-0-7864-4609-4
softcover : acid free paper ∞

1. Baseball—United States—History.
2. Baseball players—United States—Death.
3. Mays, Carl, 1891–
4. Chapman, Ray, d. 1920.
I. Title.
GV863.A1L29 2012 796.357'64097309042—dc23 2012002287

British Library cataloguing data are available

Cover illustration by Molly Lawless

Manufactured in the United States of America

McFarland & Company, Inc., Publishers
Box 611, Jefferson, North Carolina 28640
www.mcfarlandpub.com

To my father, James Lawless, who first introduced me to baseball's magic, hilarity and heartbreak.
I love you, Dad.

And to my wonderful husband, Carlton King:
I couldn't have done this without you.

Table of Contents

Preface

Hit by Pitch is based on the true story of Carl Mays, Ray Chapman, and the moment they became forever linked: a fatal pitch. I have not aimed to break new ground on this subject matter from a scholarly perspective, for no one could top Mike Sowell's book *The Pitch That Killed* in that regard. Hopefully *Hit by Pitch* will provide an accessible entry point to those interested in baseball of this era and tell this story that very few people know. Certainly any casual fan of the early-20th century game knows Ray Chapman's fate, but as a footnote to baseball, an answer to a trivia question. I hope that this book brings the full story surrounding it, and these two men, back to life. *Hit by Pitch* is episodic: I hope that many of the chapters could stand alone as vignettes. While the death of a ballplayer may not seem like a lighthearted topic, there are moments of levity here, and this book contain elements of the comedy, tragedy, and mystery that this true drama offers.

I've known of this story since I was around eight years old. When I was a rabid baseball fan growing up in Boston in the 1980's (my team was the then-hapless Red Sox), I soon found that the 162-game season was much too short for me. I needed more. My father had a small stash of baseball books, and I began poring over them with the intensity of a scholar. One of these books was an old baseball encyclopedia, long since lost, the name of which I only wish I could remember. The front cover was missing, and it was several years outdated, but much to my delight it contained exhaustive statistics all the way back to 1876. Teams had bizarre names like the Bridegrooms and the Spiders, and I found there were once franchises in Worcester, Massachusetts, Troy, New York, and Providence, Rhode Island. I felt like I had discovered a new planet.

This tome included the full roster and statistics for every year, team by team, with different symbolic citations denoting various reasons a player would have been unable to complete the season with that particular ballclub. An asterisk [*], for example, would indicate he was traded, a plus sign [+] that he suffered a season-ending injury. Then the footnote would detail where he went or the nature of the injury, and so on.

Most fascinating was the macabre cross symbol [†] that marked that the player had died during the season. The idea of this happening during the modern age seemed unthinkable, and so attached was I to my favorite players, I could barely entertain the idea of coping with one of their deaths. How could that happen? And the ways they died--suicides, gunshots, bizarre accidents, outdated diseases like consumption and dropsy—made it all the more otherworldly. The reduction of a player's death to a footnoted phrase had the terrifying deliciousness of a ghost story, and I couldn't wait to get to the bottom of the page to find out how he'd met his mortal end.

Soon I came upon the 1920 Cleveland Indians and their loss: Ray Chapman, whose "†" indicated that he had been killed by a pitched ball. That one phrase, describing a deadly moment in a long-ago game was enough to send my imagination into overdrive. Someone actually died from an injury in a major league baseball game? The story stuck with me.

My baseball obsession waned considerably over the years, but I always had a deep fondness for the dead ball era (1901–1919) and the golden age of the 1920's, these long-dead players and their stories, due in no small part, I'm sure, to bits and pieces I discovered in that encyclopedia. Then about six years ago I came across Lawrence S. Ritter's *The Glory of Their Times: The Story of the Early Days of Baseball Told by the Men Who Played It*, a wonderful collection of interviews with players from the first part of the 20th century, and my love was reborn. By this time I had begun writing and drawing my own comics. I found inspiration in these stories, illustrating a few of the tales I found in my reading in my series of one-page comics, "Great Moments in Baseball." Thus I started my baseball re-education, eventually coming to Mike Sowell's masterful *The Pitch That Killed,* which dealt exclusively with Chapman, Mays, and the 1920 season. This is an amazing story. The two main characters seem to come straight from central casting: Chapman, the fallen hero, popular and gregarious; Mays, the villain, scowling and unlikable. The setting was baseball at a transitional moment, during the breaking of the Black Sox scandal and on the threshold of a new era. The cast of supporting characters was a who's who of the era's baseball luminaries—Tris Speaker, Ty Cobb, and Babe Ruth, among others. The storybook ending—a mourning team wins their first World Series—was cinema-ready, and the tale as told by Sowell was my main inspiration. I wanted to tell this story the best way I could, through the medium of comics. I hope I've done it justice.

The book that led me to *The Pitch That Killed* was Fred Lieb's *Baseball as I Have Known It*, which included the author's fascinating firsthand account of the Chapman-Mays incident and Mays' subsequent career and the suspicions that surrounded him unrelated to Chapman's death. Much of this material is covered in my chapter "The 1921 World Series: A Drama in Three Acts."

I'd like to thank the following for their help bringing this project to life: the folks at the SABR Deadball Era Research Committee who kindly included my "Great Moments in Baseball" comics in the "Inside Game" newsletter, ultimately leading McFarland to my work; the staff of the Periodicals Room at the Library of Congress; the staff at the Baseball Hall of Fame's A. Bartlett Giamatti Research Center for their help with reference photos; and Rob Neyer for generously lending me his copy of Bob McGarigle's out-of-print and very useful Carl Mays biography, *Baseball's Great Tragedy: The Story of Carl Mays, Submarine Pitcher.*

I hope you enjoy my take on this great story.

August 16, 1920

New York, NY

Introduction.

Indians 4, Yankees 3

EVERY BASEBALL GAME IS ITS OWN DRAMA.

SOME MOMENTS FORGETTABLE AND ROUTINE....

...AND OTHERS EPIC FOR REASONS NO ONE WATCHING EVEN KNOWS YET.

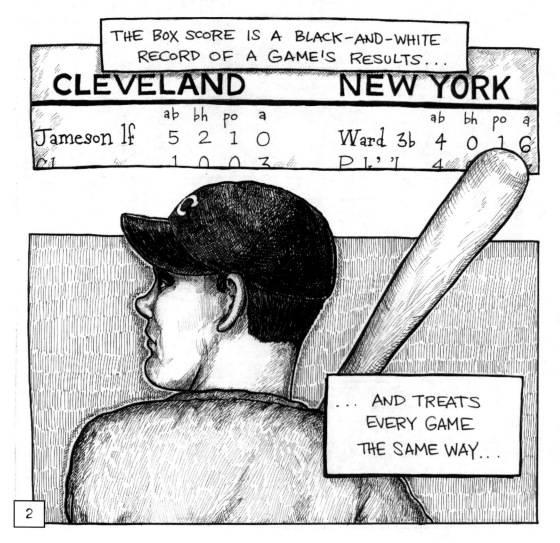

THE BOX SCORE IS A BLACK-AND-WHITE RECORD OF A GAME'S RESULTS...

CLEVELAND	ab	bh	po	a	NEW YORK	ab	bh	po	a
Jameson lf	5	2	1	0	Ward 3b	4	0	1	6

...AND TREATS EVERY GAME THE SAME WAY...

IT TALLIES THE TOTAL RUNS BY INNING...

Cleveland 0 1 0 2 1 0 0 0 0 — 4
New York 0 0 0 0 0 0 0 0 3 — 3

... AND HOW LONG THOSE NINE INNINGS TOOK.

1 hr., 55 min.

... THE PLAYERS THAT WERE ON THE FIELD THAT DAY, BOTH THOSE WHO HAVE LONG BEEN **FORGOTTEN**...

Ward 3b 4 0 1 6

... AND THOSE WELL ON THEIR WAY TO BECOMING **LEGENDS**.

Speaker cf

Ruth rf

WE LEARN WHO HAD A GOOD GAME...

O'Neill c 4 3 8 0

Ward 3b 4 0 1 6
Peck'p'h ss 4 0 3 3

... AND WHO CAME UP A **LITTLE SHORT**.

IN RETROSPECT, THE BOX SCORE REVEALS THE **FOOTNOTES OF HISTORY** WHO WERE PRESENT THAT DAY..

NY
WALLY PIPP, FIVE YEARS AWAY FROM LOSING HIS JOB AS FIRST BASEMAN TO LOU GEHRIG

... AND THOSE WHO WOULD LIVE ON AS ANSWERS TO TRIVIA QUESTIONS.
BILL WAMBSGANSS: WOULD COMPLETE THE ONLY UNASSISTED TRIPLE PLAY IN WORLD SERIES HISTORY.
Wambs's 2b

THE BOX SCORE LINES UP THE GAME'S EVENTS NEATLY, IN ROWS AND COLUMNS...

O'Neill c	4	3	8	0	Bodie cf	4	2	4	0
Johnston 1b	4	1	10	0	Ruel c	3	2	5	0
Wambs's 3b	4	0	4	2	Mays p	2	0	0	4
Coveleskie p	3	0	0	3	*Vick	1	1	0	0

... PRESERVING ITS STATISTICS FOR POSTERITY.

BUT AS ANY FAN KNOWS, IT DOESN'T TELL THE WHOLE STORY.

IN THE SPACE BETWEEN THE NAMES AND NUMBERS,

C	ab	bh	po	a	NEW YORK	ab	bh	po	a
Jameson lf	5	2	1	0	Ward 3b	4	0	1	6
Chapman ss	1	0	0	3	Peck'p'h ss	4	0	3	3
Lunte ss	1	0	0	2	Ruth rf	4	1	1	0
Speaker cf	4	0	0	0	Pratt 2b	3	1	1	4
Smith rf	4	0	2	0	Lewis lf	4	0	0	0
Gardner 3b	3	1	2	1	Pipp 1b	3	0	12	0
O'Neill c	4	3	8	0	Bodie cf	4	2	4	0
Johnston 1b	4	1	10	0	Ruel c	3	2	5	0
Wambs's 2b	4	0	4	2	Mays p	2	0	0	4
Covel'skie p	3	0	0	3	* Vick	1	1	0	0
Totals	3								

Innings 1 2 3 4 5 6 7 8 9

THE TRIUMPHS AND FAILURES,

THERE'S ALWAYS SOMETHING THE STATS MISS.

THERE'S NO COLUMN IN THE BOX SCORE THAT RECORDS THE MOOD OF THE CROWD...
MILLER HUGGINS, MANAGER
CHRIST, MY HEAD! DO THEY EVER LET UP?!
AW, HUG... GIVE 'EM A BREAK!

AND DARK! D'YOU THINK IT'LL RAIN?
SO... VERY... MUGGY...

... OR THE CONDITIONS AT THE FIELD THAT DAY...

...OR THAT THESE TWO TEAMS WERE IN THE MIDST OF A CLOSE PENNANT RACE.

THERE'S NO WAY TO TELL THAT THE GAME OF BASEBALL WOULD SOON BE IN **SERIOUS CRISIS**....

... OR THAT A MAN ON THE FIELD WOULD **SAVE** IT BY DOING THINGS NO ONE ELSE HAD **EVER** DONE.

ON AUGUST 16, 1920, THE YANKEES FACED THE INDIANS AT NEW YORK'S POLO GROUNDS...

..AND TO LOOK AT THE BOX SCORE, IT WAS MUCH LIKE COUNTLESS BALLGAMES PLAYED BOTH BEFORE IT AND SINCE.

THERE'S NO PLACE ON A BOX SCORE TO RECORD A **FATAL INJURY** SUFFERED ON A BASEBALL DIAMOND--

Mays 3, Covaleskie 4. Hit by pitched ball — By Mays (Chapman.)

BECAUSE IT'S ONLY HAPPENED **ONCE**.

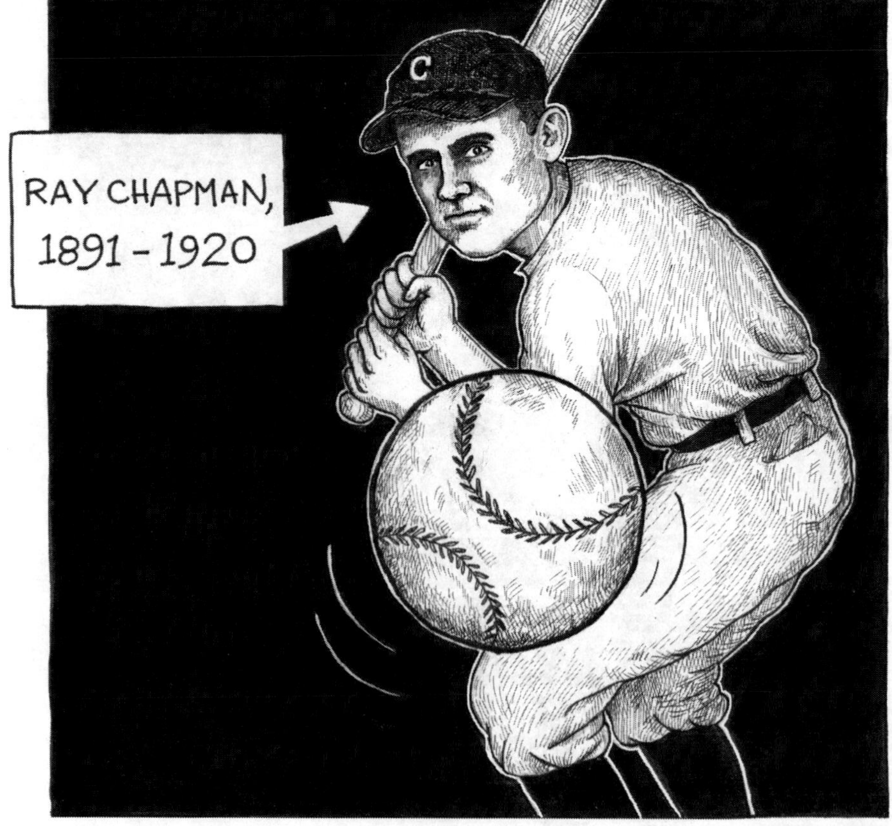

CLEVELAND	ab	bh	po	a	NEW YORK	ab	bh	po	a
Jameson lf	5	2	1	0	Ward 3b	4	0	1	6
Chapman ss	1	0	0	3	Peck'p'h ss	4	0	3	3
Lunte ss	1	0	0	2	Ruth rf	4	1	1	0
Speaker cf	4	0	0	0	Pratt 2b	3	1	1	4
Smith rf	4	0	2	0	Lewis lf	4	0	0	0
Gardner 3b	3	1	2	1	Pipp 1b	3	0	12	0
O'Neill c	4	3	8	0	Bodie cf	4	2	4	0
Johnston 1b	4	1	10	0	Ruel c	3	2	5	0
Wambs's 2b	4	0	4	2	Mays p	2	0	0	4
Covel'skie p	3	0	0	3	*Vick	1	1	0	0
					Thorm'len p	0	0	0	0
					†O'Doul	1	0	0	0
Totals	33	1	27	12	Totals	33	7	27	17

Innings	1	2	3	4	5	6	7	8	9	
Cleveland	0	1	0	2	1	0	0	0	0	—4
New York	0	0	0	0	0	0	0	0	3	—3

Errors — Ward, Ruel. Two-base hit — Bodie. Home run — O'Neill. Double play — Pipp (unassisted). Base on balls — Off Mays 1, Covaleskie 2. Struck out — By Mays 3, Covaleskie 4. Hit by pitched ball — By Mays (Chapman.) Umpires — Connolly (plate) and Nailin. Time — 1 hr. 55 min.

* Batted for Mays in 8th.

† Batted for Thormahlen in 9th.

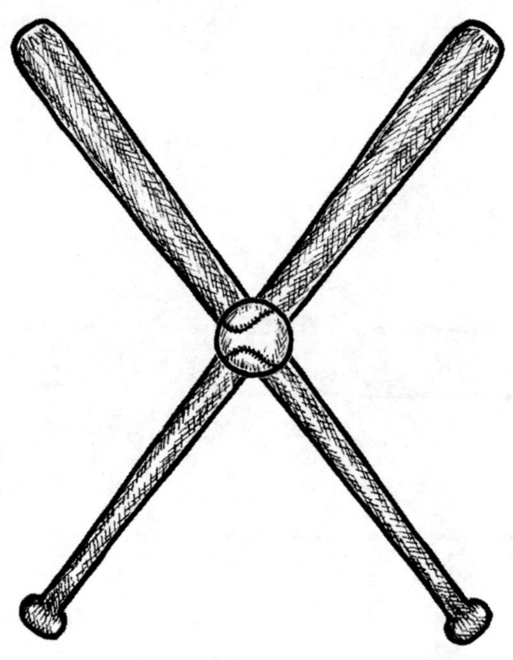

Part I

Origins.

1

KENTUCKY, 1891

RAYMOND JOHNSON CHAPMAN, BORN JANUARY 15.

LIBERTY

BEAVER DAM

CARL WILLIAM MAYS, BORN NOVEMBER 12.

IT ALL BEGAN (WELL, FOR **RAY CHAPMAN** AND **CARL MAYS**, THAT IS) IN 1891 WHEN, TEN MONTHS AND 150 MILES APART, THE TWO MEN WERE BORN.

BUT NEITHER WAS IN KENTUCKY LONG. BY 1905, BOTH FAMILIES HAD LEFT IT BEHIND IN FAVOR OF BETTER PROSPECTS **ELSEWHERE**.

FOR THE CHAPMANS, THAT WAS HERRIN, ILLINOIS, WHERE RAY'S FATHER EVERETTE FOUND WORK AS A MINER.

AND FOR THE MAYS, IT WAS MANSFIELD, MISSOURI, WHERE WILLIAM MAYS, CARL'S FATHER, SERVED AS A TRAVELING MINISTER.

BOTH FAMILIES EXPERIENCED THEIR SHARE OF HARDSHIPS IN THOSE DIFFICULT DAYS IN THE RURAL MIDWEST.

RAY'S BROTHER ROY BECAME ILL WITH SPINAL MENINGITIS AS A BABY AND WOULD NEVER WALK OR TALK WITHOUT DIFFICULTY.

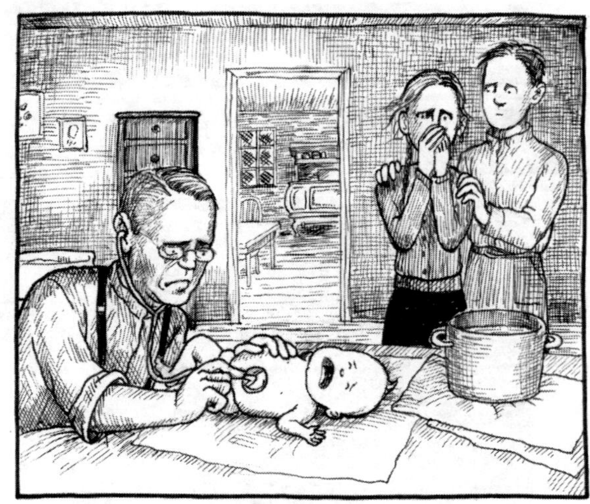

AND WHEN CARL WAS TEN, HIS FATHER DIED SUDDENLY FROM A FEVER, SAID TO BE A RESULT OF GETTING CAUGHT IN A RAINSTORM AFTER A PARTICULARLY **TAXING** PREACHING SESSION.

BOTH BOYS WORKED TO HELP SUPPORT THEIR FAMILIES AS SOON AS THEY WERE ABLE.

RAY DELIVERED GROCERIES, AND SOMETIMES JOINED HIS DAD IN THE MINES.

CARL TENDED TO ALL SORTS OF CHORES ON HIS FAMILY'S FARM.

IT WAS AROUND THIS TIME THAT EACH HELD A BASEBALL FOR THE **VERY FIRST TIME**...

...AND BEFORE THEY WERE OUT OF THEIR TEENS, THEY WERE BEING **PAID** TO **PLAY**.

2

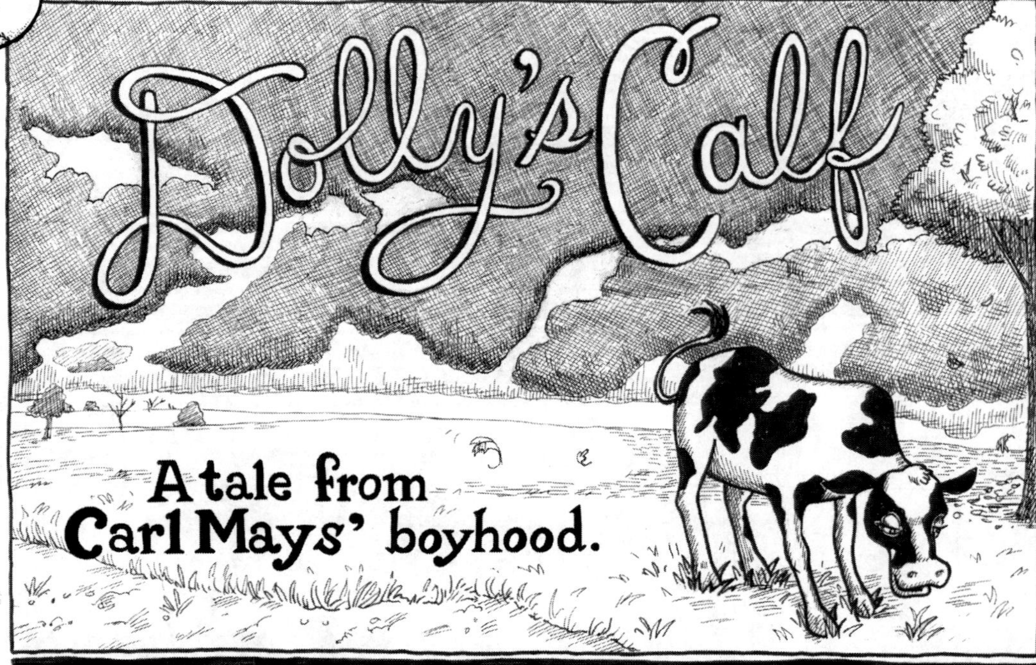

Dolly's Calf
A tale from Carl Mays' boyhood.

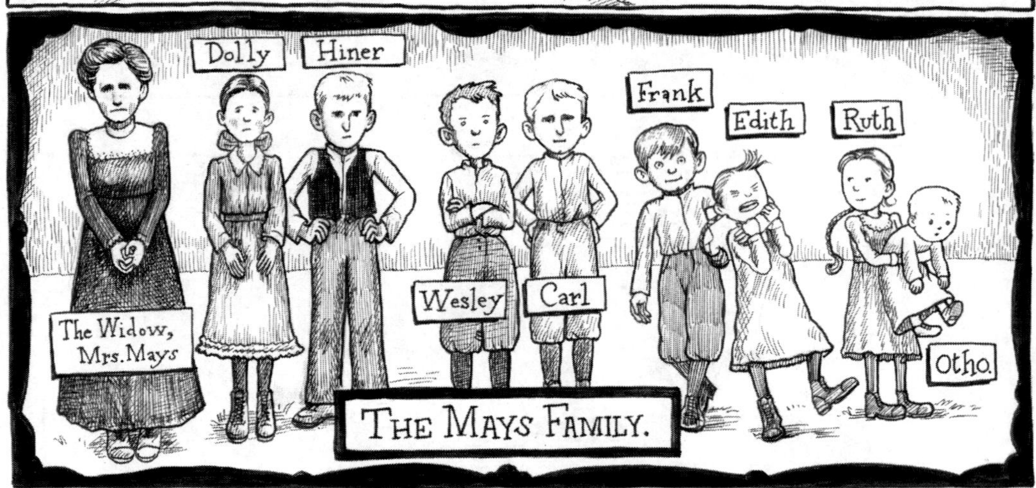

Wesley and Carl were making their way home from gathering hickory nuts one cloudy October day...

I'VE GOT MORE NUTS THAN YOU.
SO?

CARL, DID YOU JUST HIT ANOTHER SQUIRREL?
YUP.

HEY, IS THAT DOLLY'S CALF OVER THERE?

YEP, THAT'S HER!

BETCHA I CAN MAKE HER JUMP.
crack
OH YEAH? HOW ARE YOU GONNA DO THAT?

WHY, I'LL HIT HER ON THE RUMP!
YOU'RE CRAZY! SHE'S TOO FAR AWAY.

NO, SHE'S NOT.
YES, SHE IS.

IS NOT!
IS TOO!

OKAY, WESLEY.
HMMM....
I'LL BET YOU MY WHOLE BAG OF NUTS I CAN REACH HER.

YOU'RE ON.

JUST PICK A ROCK, ALREADY!
I WANT TO COLLECT MY WINNINGS.
YAAAAAWN...
THIS ONE SHOULD DO IT...

OOPS.

OH, **LORDY**, CARL! LOOK WHAT YOU DID!
SHE'S **DEAD**, WES.

WHAT ARE WE GONNA **DO**?!

LET ME THINK...

OKAY.

WE'LL BURY HER.

BUT FIRST, WE'LL SKIN HER AND SELL THE HIDE.

GO GET A SHOVEL.

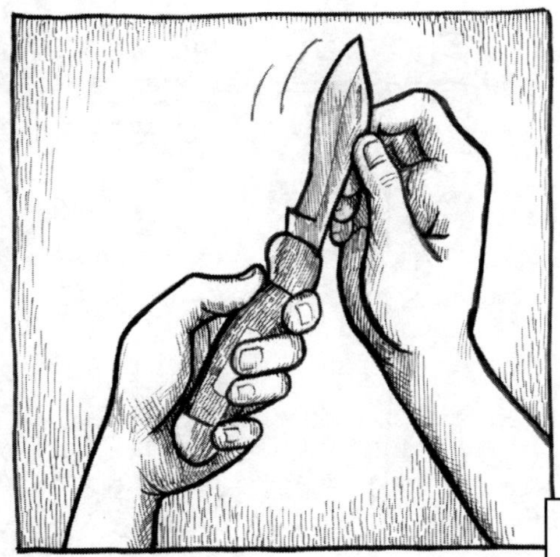

THERE.

NOW, OFF TO THE STORE. FORGET THE SHOVELS-- WE'LL COME BACK FOR 'EM LATER.

TOWE'S GENERAL STORE

HOWDY, MR. TOWE!

HOWDY, BOYS!
WHAT'VE YOU GOT THERE?

A HIDE.
THOUGHT YOU MIGHT LIKE TO BUY IT. ONLY THIRTY-FIVE CENTS!

HMM... IT'S AWFULLY SMALL.
HOW ABOUT TWENTY-FIVE?

SOLD!

C·A·N·D·Y

GOBBLE GOBBLE

That evening, at dinner...
CARL AND WESLEY, YOU'VE BARELY TOUCHED YOUR SUPPER!

I'M JUST NOT HUNGRY.
WE ATE A LOT OF... UM... HICKORY NUTS.

REALLY?
I TALKED TO MR. TOWE AT THE STORE TODAY...

HE SAID YOU SOLD HIM A HIDE THIS AFTERNOON.
DOLLY, WILL YOU TAKE OTHO, PLEASE?

AND THAT YOU SPENT ALL THE MONEY ON CANDY.
CARL, WESLEY... DID YOU... KILL DOLLY'S CALF?
GASP!

IT WAS AN ACCIDENT.

Carl & The Babe

IN 1914, CARL MAYS AND BABE RUTH CAME UP FROM THE MINORS TOGETHER... LITERALLY.

HEY! WE'RE ON THE SAME TRAIN!
UGH.
LOOKS LIKE IT.
ALL RIGHT!
PROVIDENCE TO BOSTON... ALL ABOOAAARD!

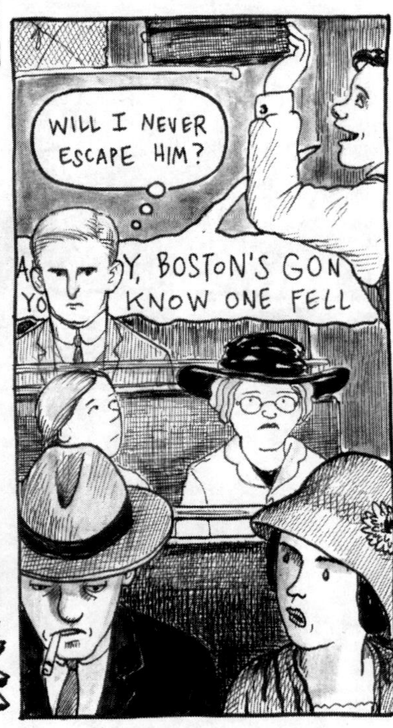
WILL I NEVER ESCAPE HIM?
Y, BOSTON'S GON
KNOW ONE FELL

I'M GETTIN' A DRINK. WANT ONE?
IT'S EIGHT-THIRTY IN THE MORNING.
IS THAT A NO? HA! MORE FOR ME.

CARL, DID YOU SEE THE BOTTOM ON HER? JESUS!
DO YOU EVER STOP?
STOP WHAT?

They would remain teammates --never friends -- on the Red Sox and Yankees for the next eight years.

4

OUR MAN "CHAPPIE"!
EXTRA!

Just How Popular IS This Chapman Fellow, Anyway?

I'M GLAD YOU ASKED! ED BANG HERE, CLEVELAND NEWS- AND I'VE GOT AN EXCLUSIVE!

HE MAY BE A KENTUCKY BOY BY BIRTH...
CLEVELAND
... BUT RAY CHAPMAN IS CLEVELAND'S FAVORITE SON NOW!

FRIENDS, YOU'VE SEEN HIM WORK HIS MAGIC ON THE FIELD, BUT I'M HERE TO TELL YOU:
OH, CHAPMAN!
HE'S AS MUCH AT HOME IN THE BALLROOM AS THE BALL DIAMOND!

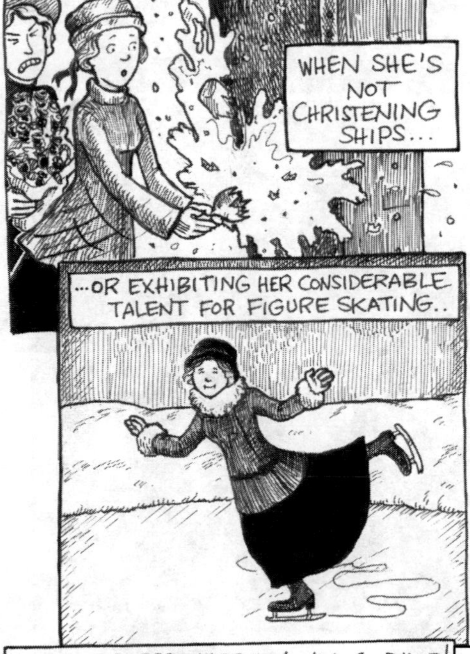

NOW, I IMAGINE MANY OF YOU ARE FAMILIAR WITH A MISS KATHLEEN DALY FROM THE SOCIETY PAGES.
WHEN SHE'S NOT CHRISTENING SHIPS...
...OR EXHIBITING HER CONSIDERABLE TALENT FOR FIGURE SKATING..
...JUST GUESS WHERE YOU'LL FIND HER!

THIS SOCIALITE ENJOYS NOTHING MORE THAN A **DAY** AT THE **BALLPARK** WITH HER FATHER, EAST OHIO GAS COMPANY PRESIDENT (AND SELF-MADE MILLIONAIRE), MARTIN DALY.

DADDY, THAT CHAPMAN FELLOW SEEMS NICE...
...DON'T YOU THINK?
HMMM..

I HEAR THAT SHE CAN EVEN SCORE THE GAMES HERSELF – A **RARE PURSUIT** FOR THE FAIRER SEX.

MY FRIENDS, OUR CHAPPIE KNOWS A **GEM** WHEN HE SEES ONE, AND THAT A YOUNG LADY WHO SO LOVES SPENDING TIME AT THE DIAMOND...

WILL YOU...
OF COURSE!

..CERTAINLY DESERVES ONE OF HER **OWN**!

THEIR WEDDING WAS **QUITE** THE EVENT HERE IN CLEVELAND...

ASSORTED BALLPLAYERS AND LOCAL GLITTERATI
CLEVELAND MAYOR HARRY DAVIS
ME, ED BANG.
The Happy Couple!

... AND MR. CHAPMAN BOASTED NONE OTHER THAN "THE GRAY EAGLE" HIMSELF – TEAMMATE AND MANAGER **TRIS SPEAKER** – AS HIS **BEST MAN**.

TRIS
TRIS'S GIRLFRIEND (AND KATHLEEN'S COUSIN AND BRIDESMAID)

SPEAKING OF "SPOKE"...

...THIS WILL BE HIS FIRST FULL SEASON AT THE HELM OF THE SQUAD, IN ADDITION TO HIS CUSTOMARY CENTERFIELDING DUTIES.
AND I CAN REPORT WITH CERTAINTY THAT THERE'S NOTHING CHAPPIE WOULD LIKE MORE THAN TO DELIVER A CHAMPIONSHIP FOR HIS "SKIPPER" AND BEST MAN - NOT TO MENTION US!

HOWEVER, IN ADDITION TO BASEBALL AND HIS NEW BRIDE, THERE ARE FURTHER CONSTRAINTS ON RAY'S TIME THESE DAYS.
CLEVELAND, OHIO
MY OWN OFFICE - HOW DO YOU LIKE THAT?
IN THE OFF-SEASON, HE'S BECOME QUITE THE BUSINESSMAN. AS THE TREASURER-SECRETARY OF PIONEER ALLOYS, OUR SHORTSTOP IS MOVING UP IN THE WORLD!

MR. DALY HAS BEEN KNOWN TO SAY THAT HE'S GAINED A NEW SON-IN-LAW AND BUSINESS PARTNER.
IN FACT, HE'S SHOWN SUCH PROMISE IN THIS CAPACITY, THERE ARE RUMBLINGS THAT CHAPMAN PLANS TO RETIRE AFTER THIS SEASON.

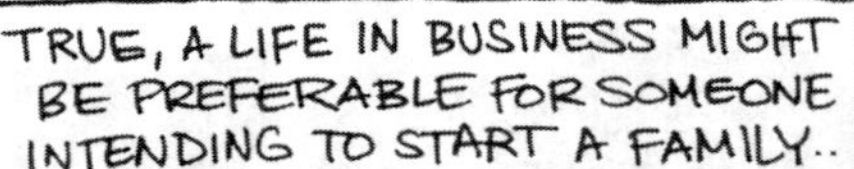

Jack Graney, teammate

...ESPECIALLY A LARGE ONE.

BUT HOW COULD IT BE? CHAPPIE LEAVING HIS TEAM—AND FANS!—TO BECOME A CAPTAIN OF INDUSTRY?

I KNOW THAT ALL OF CLEVELAND WOULD SHUDDER AT THE THOUGHT.

WE CAN ONLY HOPE THAT HE RECONSIDERS, OR THAT SPEAKER, GRANEY, AND THE BOYS CAN CONVINCE HIM TO HANG AROUND.

IF, HOWEVER, THIS UNFORTUNATE EVENT DOES OCCUR AND WE DO LOSE OUR STAR SHORTSTOP, CLEVELAND BASEBALL'S LOSS WILL BE A GAIN FOR CLEVELAND'S BUSINESS. FOR IT SEEMS THAT WHEREVER CHAPPIE GOES, HE'S SURE TO IMPRESS AND DELIGHT EVERYONE HE MEETS.

BACK IN SEMIPRO, FOR EXAMPLE, HE QUICKLY MADE HIS MARK...

RAY? OH, YOU MEAN CHAPPIE! SURE...
A JOLLY GUY. ALWAYS LAUGHING, TALKING, SINGING...
AN OLD TEAMMATE
KID, EVEN IF YOU NEVER PLAYED A GAME, YOU'D EARN YOUR PAY BEING SUCH A CHEERLEADER!
MANAGER
SPRINGFIELD
YEAH!
THAT'S THE STUFF!

HE DIDN'T GET MUCH ON-FIELD ACTION AT FIRST, BUT WAS STILL A VALUABLE COMMODITY.

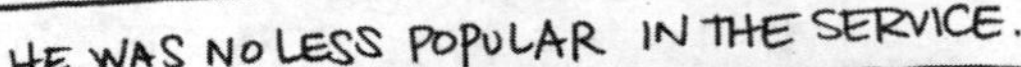

HE WAS NO LESS POPULAR IN THE SERVICE.

"CHAPPIE" ALWAYS ACTED A GENTLEMAN AND ENDEARED HIMSELF TO EVERY GOB AND OFFICER ON THE SHIP.
COMMANDING OFFICER IN NAVAL RESERVES, 1918

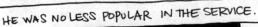

YES, THEY'VE ALL GOT STARS IN THEIR EYES WHEN THEY TALK OF OUR CHAPPIE. AND I SUSPECT YOU'VE HEARD OF THESE THREE FELLOWS:

THEY COUNT THEMSELVES AMONG HIS FRIENDS AND ADMIRERS TOO.

YES, HE'S GOT FANS AND ADMIRERS FROM ACROSS THE SPECTRUM....
EXTRA!
SPORTS
Chapman saves day for Indians!
CHAPPIE DOES IT AGAIN!
A FINE SHORTSTOP, AND AN EVEN FINER MAN!
Mayor Davis
...BECAUSE HE'S ALWAYS HIMSELF, WITH NO FRILLS OR FURBELOWS.

BUT WHAT'S **MOST STRIKING** ABOUT CHAPPIE'S WINNING PERSONALITY IS HIS EFFECT ON THE TEAM'S **MORALE.**

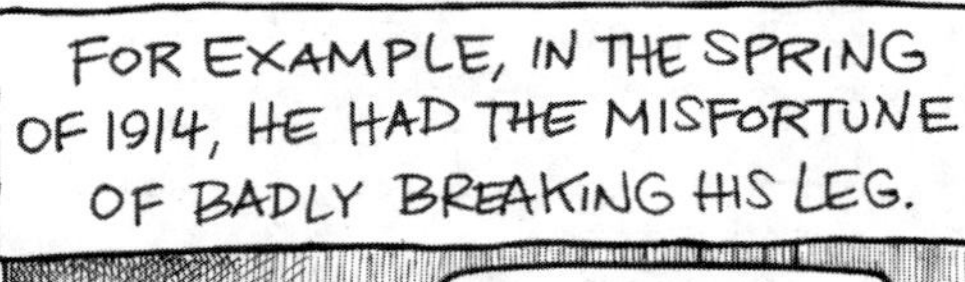

FOR EXAMPLE, IN THE SPRING OF 1914, HE HAD THE MISFORTUNE OF BADLY BREAKING HIS LEG.

I WANTED TO BE THE BEST SHORTSTOP IN AMERICA!

HE HAD ONLY PLAYED ONE FULL SEASON WITH THE CLUB, BUT WHAT HAPPENED TO THEM WHILE HE WAS OUT WAS A **SAD SIGHT INDEED**.

AS A FELLOW SPORTSWRITER SAID, "IT WAS THE MOST DISCOURAGED AGGREGATION OF BALL PLAYERS I EVER SAW, AND REMAINED THAT WAY UNTIL CHAPMAN REJOINED THE TEAM."

WHICH IS WHY I **SINCERELY** HOPE THAT OUR CHAPPIE STICKS WITH BASEBALL--AND THE CLEVELAND SQUAD.

~SEASON 1920~

FOR AS TALENTED AND DETERMINED AS THESE BOYS ARE, I JUST DON'T KNOW HOW THEY'D GET ALONG WITHOUT HIM!

5

RAY CHAPMAN: "FAMED IRISH TENOR"

ONE WINTER, CHAPPIE'S BUDDY JOHN ALEXANDER WAS ENTERTAINING A GROUP OF FRIENDS AT HIS HOME, WOWING THEM WITH HIS STATE-OF-THE-ART PHONOGRAPH SET-UP AND EXTENSIVE COLLECTION OF RECORDINGS.

THEY WERE ENJOYING A SONG BY JOHN McCORMACK (FAMED IRISH TENOR) WHEN CHAPPIE SHOWED UP. IT JUST SO HAPPENED THAT NONE OF ALEXANDER'S GUESTS HAD MET CHAPPIE BEFORE, SO HE COOKED UP A LITTLE PRANK.

HEY-O, ALL! WHAT ARE WE UP TO?

WHAT AN INCREDIBLE COINCIDENCE!
?
HAVE I GOT A SURPRISE FOR ALL OF YOU! MY DEAR FRIEND — THE TENOR HIMSELF — JOHN McCORMACK!

THEY LOOKED NOTHING ALIKE, BUT ALEXANDER TOOK A CHANCE AND ASSUMED NONE OF HIS FRIENDS HAD ANY IDEA WHAT THE REAL SINGER LOOKED LIKE. HE WAS RIGHT.

HE ATTEMPTED TO DEMUR, BUT THEY WERE **INSISTENT**.

WHEN HIS KNOWLEDGE OF THE McCORMACK OEUVRE WAS EXHAUSTED, THE PERFORMANCE WAS FINALLY OVER . . .

... UNTIL NEWS SPREAD THROUGH TOWN THAT THE "FAMOUS TENOR" WAS IN TOWN GIVING IMPROMPTU SHOWS.

AND THAT'S WHEN THE REQUESTS FOR MORE CONCERTS BEGAN COMING IN.

6

COLLISION COURSE

HE DRAPED HIMSELF OVER THE PLATE. I ALWAYS **DREADED** PITCHING TO HIM.

Mays On Chapman.

HE THROWS SO HE'LL DUST YOU OFF THE PLATE. BUT HE'S NOT GOING TO INTIMIDATE **ME**!

Chapman On Mays.

Their origins and the game they played aside, these two were about as different as they could be.

CHAPMAN MADE HIS MAJOR LEAGUE DEBUT IN 1912, AND SOON BECAME A FIXTURE IN THE CLEVELAND INFIELD. HITTING WAS NEVER HIS STRENGTH, BUT HIS BLISTERING SPEED AND EXCELLENT FIELDING MORE THAN MADE UP FOR IT. AFTER SUFFERING INJURIES THAT SHORTENED HIS 1914 AND 1916 SEASONS, HE REALLY HIT HIS STRIDE IN 1917. HE HIT .302, STOLE 52 BASES (A TEAM RECORD) AND IN ADDITION SET AN ALL-TIME RECORD FOR SACRIFICE BUNTS IN A SEASON WITH 67.

"CHAPPIE" SPEEDS UP CLEVELAND OFFENSE

CARL MAYS: "PINCH PITCHER" OF THE WORLD CHAMPIONS.

MAYS PITCHED HIS FIRST GAME WITH THE BOSTON RED SOX IN 1915. BY 1917, HE TOO WAS COMING INTO HIS OWN — AS ONE OF BASEBALL'S PREMIER PITCHERS, WITH A 22-9 RECORD. THIS SEASON HIGHLIGHTED A CURIOUS DICHOTOMY IN MAYS' PITCHING. HIS RATIO OF WALKED BATTERS PER GAME WAS THE LEAGUE'S LOWEST, INDICATING EXCELLENT CONTROL. YET AT THE SAME TIME, HE LED THE LEAGUE IN HIT BATSMEN. THIS SEEMED TO CONFIRM WHAT MANY BATTERS WHO HAD BEEN VICTIMS OF HIS ERRANT PITCHES CLAIMED THROUGHOUT HIS CAREER: WHEN MAYS HIT YOU, IT WAS NO ACCIDENT.

AS A RESULT, EVEN AS HIS PITCHING STAR ROSE, HE WAS QUICKLY BECOMING ONE OF THE MOST UNPOPULAR PLAYERS IN BASEBALL. THIS REPUTATION EXTENDED TO HIS OWN TEAMMATES, WHO UNIFORMLY FOUND HIM **UNBEARABLE**.

HE WAS **SULKY**.
HE WAS **NOT CONGENIAL**.

HE WAS AN **ODD BIRD**.

IT WAS LIKE HE ALWAYS HAD A **TOOTHACHE**.

I'VE NEVER PLAYED WITH A FELLOW THAT WAS DISLIKED AS MUCH AS MAYS.

SPORTSWRITER F.C. LANE SUMMED IT UP THUSLY:

MAYS IS A STRANGE, CYNICAL FIGURE...
...VIRTUALLY **FRIENDLESS**.

IN THIS RESPECT, RAY CHAPMAN WAS EVERYTHING CARL MAYS WASN'T. "CHAPPIE" POSITIVELY EXUDED CHARISMA, IN A WAY THAT PROBABLY SEEMED QUITE UNFAIR TO A MAN LIKE MAYS.

HIS TEAMMATES FELL ALL OVER EACH OTHER TO GET CLOSE TO HIM.

HE WAS NO STRANGER TO THE LOCAL NIGHTLIFE, AND HE AND THREE TEAMMATES STARTED A SINGING GROUP THAT PERFORMED AROUND CLEVELAND. HE BECAME A FAN FAVORITE, ESPECIALLY ONCE HE CEMENTED HIS ALLEGIANCE TO THE TOWN WHEN HE MARRIED KATY IN 1919.

HE WAS ALMOST ALWAYS CHEERFUL. HE ONCE (UNCHARACTERISTICALLY) ARGUED WITH AN UMPIRE* OVER A CALL THAT DIDN'T GO HIS WAY...

BILL, I GUESS YOU WIN THAT ONE. LOOKS LIKE I WAS WRONG.

...THEN APPROACHED HIM LATER TO MAKE AMENDS. "IT TOOK A REAL FELLOW TO DO THAT," THE UMPIRE REFLECTED.

*BILLY EVANS

His grace at shortstop garnered comparisons to the all-time great at that position, Honus Wagner.

The Flying Dutchman?
Me?
Aw, you're making me blush.

His fielding was like his personality: **entertaining and effortless.**

Mays' ballplaying style mirrored his disposition, too: **awkward** and **weird.** His delivery, while effective, was hardly **poetry in motion.**

In fact, it was downright **painful** looking. Baseball Magazine described the sight of Mays on the mound as "a cross between an **octopus and a bowler**."

AT THE END OF THE WAR-SHORTENED 1918 SEASON BOTH MEN SPENT TIME IN THE ARMED FORCES... AND ONCE AGAIN, THEIR EXPERIENCES WERE ALMOST RIDICULOUSLY DIVERGENT.

CHAPMAN ENLISTED IN THE NAVAL RESERVE AS A SECOND-CLASS SEAMAN.

WHETHER SERVING AS CAPTAIN OF THE SQUAD'S BASEBALL AND FOOTBALL TEAMS, WINNING FOOTRACES, OR SAILING THE GREAT LAKES, HIS TIME IN THE SERVICE WAS AN EXTENDED FIELD DAY.

HE DESCRIBED IT AS "ONE OF THE GREATEST EXPERIENCES OF [HIS] LIFE."

MAYS WAS ON TOP OF THE WORLD AFTER PITCHING – AND WINNING! – THE DECIDING GAME OF THE 1918 WORLD SERIES FOR THE RED SOX.

...AND GETTING MARRIED TO MARJORIE FREDERICKA ("FREDDIE") MADDEN JUST A WEEK LATER.

AFTER A FEW DAYS OF HONEYMOONING, HE RECEIVED HIS MARCHING ORDERS. HE AND HIS FELLOW DRAFTEES HEADED TO ST. LOUIS FOR THEIR TRAINING.

THEY ARRIVED JUST AS THE INFLUENZA EPIDEMIC WAS PEAKING. A FEW OF THEM FELL ILL ALMOST IMMEDIATELY, AND ALL EIGHTEEN OF THEM WERE QUARANTINED.

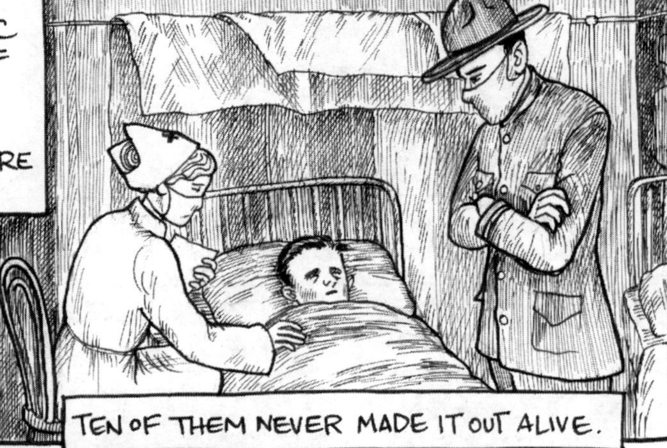

TEN OF THEM NEVER MADE IT OUT ALIVE.

MAYS WAS STILL IN ISOLATION WHEN THE ARMISTICE WAS SIGNED. WHEN HE DID FINALLY EMERGE, THE WAR WAS OVER, BUT THE EXPERIENCE HAD TAKEN A HEAVY TOLL. AS HE LATER RECALLED, "THAT HAS TO BE THE SADDEST AND MOST ILL-FATED TRIP I EVER TOOK IN ALL MY YEARS OF TRAVEL."

BY 1919, A PENNANT FINALLY SEEMED LIKE A NOT-TOO-DISTANT POSSIBILITY FOR CHAPMAN'S INDIANS. THE TEAM HAD BEEN IMPROVING STEADILY SINCE ACQUIRING TRIS SPEAKER AND OTHER KEY PLAYERS. THE ADORATION OF HIS ADOPTED CITY AND TEAMMATES, PROFESSIONAL SUCCESS, NEWLY MARRIED AND IN LOVE...

... CHAPPIE HAD IT ALL. HIS ONLY COMPLAINT WAS THAT HE MISSED HIS WIFE WHILE ON THE ROAD.

MEANWHILE, CARL MAYS WAS IMPLODING. HE AND HIS WIFE HAD NO SOONER MOVED THEIR POSSESSIONS INTO THE HOUSE HE HAD BUILT IN MANSFIELD, MASSACHUSETTS WHEN IT BURNED TO THE GROUND...

... UNDER WHAT HE WAS CONVINCED WERE SUSPICIOUS CIRCUMSTANCES.

THEN, DURING A ROWDY GAME IN PHILADELPHIA, MAYS THREW A BALL INTO THE STANDS IN ANGER, HITTING A SPECTATOR IN THE HEAD. A WARRANT WAS ISSUED FOR HIS ARREST, AND AS A RESULT HE WASN'T ABLE TO PLAY IN PHILLY FOR SEVERAL MONTHS WITHOUT FEAR OF BEING JAILED. THE RED SOX WERE SLUMPING BADLY...

.. ESPECIALLY, IT SEEMED, WHEN MAYS WAS PITCHING.

WHEN, DURING ANOTHER GAME, HIS CATCHER HIT HIM ON THE BACK OF THE HEAD WHILE TRYING TO THROW OUT A BASERUNNER, MAYS HAD REACHED HIS LIMIT.

I'LL NEVER PITCH FOR THIS CLUB AGAIN!
AND HE DIDN'T.

HE DESERTED THE RED SOX AND THE RESULT WAS AN UGLY BATTLE THAT ALMOST **TORE APART** THE AMERICAN LEAGUE. THE LEAGUE'S PRESIDENT, BAN JOHNSON, WAS CONVINCED THAT MAYS' WALKOUT-- IF IT WENT UNPUNISHED -- WOULD CREATE A STATE OF **ANARCHY**. HE WANTED MAYS SUSPENDED, AND DIDN'T WANT THE RED SOX TO TRADE HIM UNTIL THE SUSPENSION WAS SERVED. TEAM OWNERS AROUND THE LEAGUE WERE **SPLIT** OVER WHETHER JOHNSON WAS OVERREACHING HIS POWERS. FINALLY, THE **RED SOX** AND **YANKEES** **PULLED A DEAL** BEHIND JOHNSON'S BACK, TAKING OUT A SERIES OF COURT ORDERS TO KEEP HIM FROM INTERFERING, AND **SHUTTING OUT** ALL OTHER INTERESTED BALLCLUBS.

AFTER THREE WEEKS OF RIDING OUT THE STORM IN SECLUSION, CARL MAYS WAS A NEW YORK YANKEE.

WHICH BRINGS US TO 1920, THE YEAR THAT THESE TWO MEN, BORN 150 MILES APART...

... THE **LONER** AND THE **DARLING**...

... THE **BRUSHBACK ARTIST** AND THE **PLATE CROWDER**...

... ONE MAN ALREADY CONSIDERED A **VILLAIN**, THE OTHER A SAINT... COLLIDED IN A WAY THAT, LOOKING BACK, SEEMS **INEVITABLE**.

Part II

1920.

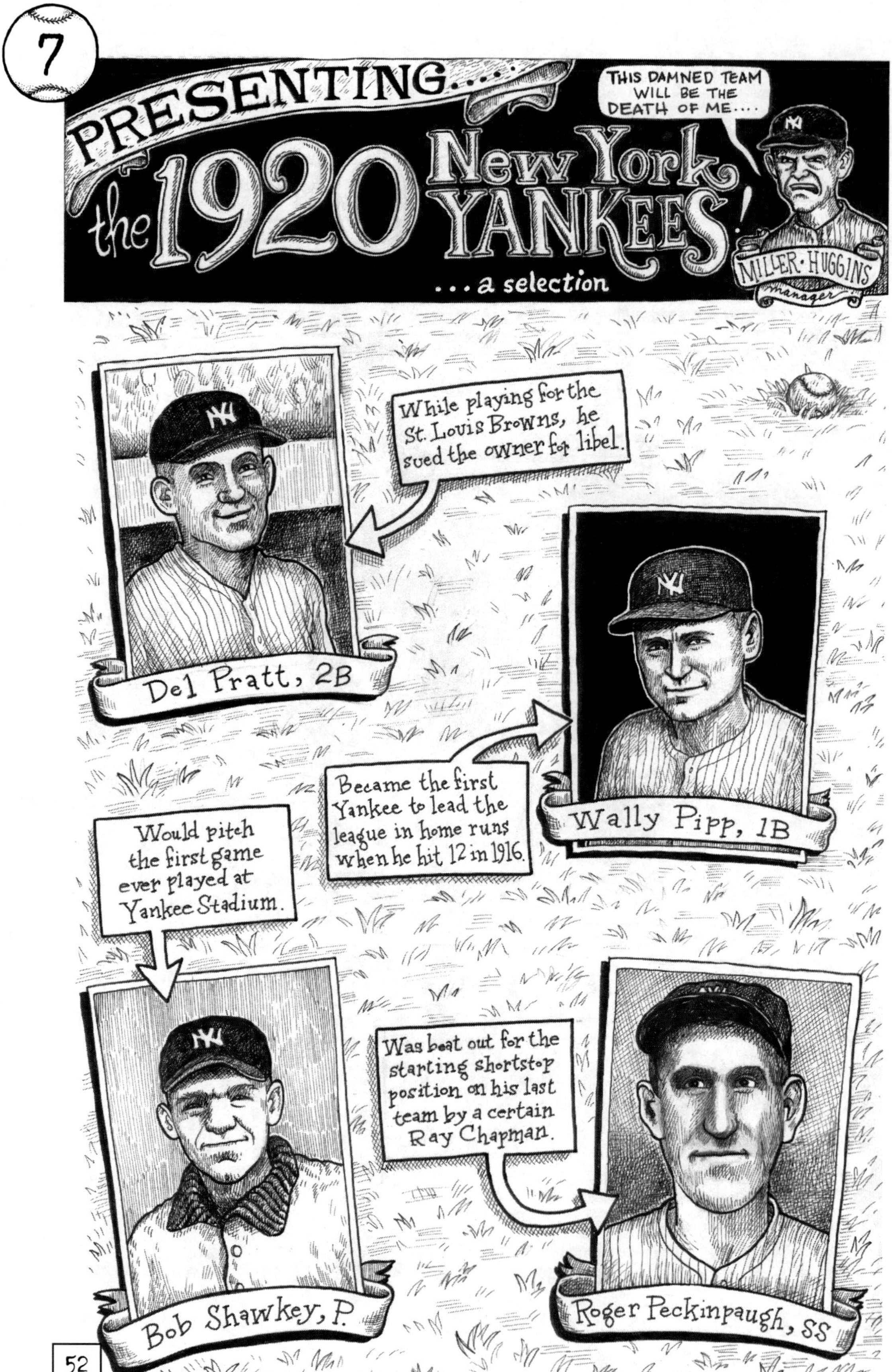

7

PRESENTING.... the 1920 New York YANKEES!

...a selection

THIS DAMNED TEAM WILL BE THE DEATH OF ME....

MILLER·HUGGINS manager

While playing for the St. Louis Browns, he sued the owner for libel.

Del Pratt, 2B

Became the first Yankee to lead the league in home runs when he hit 12 in 1916.

Wally Pipp, 1B

Would pitch the first game ever played at Yankee Stadium.

Was beat out for the starting shortstop position on his last team by a certain Ray Chapman.

Muddy Ruel, Catcher
Holds a law degree -- just like manager Miller Huggins.
"I don't room with Babe Ruth, I room with his suitcase."
Ping Bodie, 3B
George Herman "Babe" Ruth, RF
First year both with the Yankees & as a full-time outfielder. "Ruth made a grave mistake when he gave up pitching. [H]e might have... become a great star." –Tris Speaker
Before the Green Monster, Fenway Park was home to "Duffy's Cliff", as it was known during his tenure with the Red Sox.
Duffy Lewis, LF
Carl Mays, P.
With his lifetime .268 batting average, he was a pretty good hitter... ...for a pitcher.

8

PRESENTING… the 1920 Cleveland INDIANS!

…a selection

PLAY AND MANAGE? EH… I DON'T THINK SO.

TRIS SPEAKER, centerfielder …and manager.

Struck by lightning while pitching his first home game for the Indians…and still finished the game.

He and James, Jr: the first father/son duo to both pitch in the World Series.

Rhymes with "pants"

Would become baseball's first player-turned-game announcer.

"Lord, baseball is a worrying thing."

Insisted on batting seventh, as it was his favorite number.
Wheeler R. "Doc" Johnston, 1B
His birthplace is a registered historic site in Enosburg Falls, Vermont.
Larry Gardner, 3B
Tenth of thirteen children, two others of whom became big league ballplayers.
Steve O'Neill, C.
Oh, what can you say about Chappie?
Raymond Chapman, SS

9

Tris Speaker
Manliest of Men*

WELCOME TO CLEVELAND...
O·H·I·O
TRISTRAM E. SPEAKER
And what does the "E" stand for? Absolutely nothing! He made it up.
...WHERE WE'RE CURRENTLY ENJOYING THE SERVICES OF TEXAS' FINEST EXPORT! OUR PLAYER-MANAGER IS A BONA-FIDE STAR... AND GET A LOAD OF HIS TALL TALE OF A BIOGRAPHY...

* Actual description of Speaker by clearly besotted sportswriter.

BORN IN 1888, SMACK-DAB IN THE MIDDLE OF THE LONE STAR STATE...

HUBBARD CITY

YEE HAW!

... HE WAS RIDING HORSES BAREBACK WHILE STILL IN DIAPERS,

RAN AN OIL RIG ON HIS OWN WHEN HE WAS ELEVEN, AND MARAUDED THE STREETS OF HUBBARD CITY WITH A SIX SHOOTER "AS BIG AS HE WAS."

A THROW FROM A HORSE BROKE HIS RIGHT ARM AND COLLARBONE — THE DOCTOR, HE SAYS, WANTED TO AMPUTATE — BUT HE MANAGED TO TEACH HIMSELF TO BAT AND THROW LEFT-HANDED... AND HE STILL DOES TODAY.

OKAY..
THIS ISN'T SO HARD.

MISHAPS WITH BRONCOS WERE RARE. HE'S SUCH A GOOD RODEO COWBOY THAT WILL ROGERS HAS CONVINCED HIM TO ROPE 'EM IN HIS SHOW...

...BASEBALL SCHEDULE PERMITTING, OF COURSE.

AND HE'S A AN AVID ALLIGATOR WRANGLER!*

*NOT REALLY... JUST SOME SPRING TRAINING TOMFOOLERY.

IN HIS TYPICAL "GO BIG OR GO HOME" STYLE, SPOKE SOUGHT (AND ATTAINED) A SPOT IN AN ELITE AVIATION UNIT AT M.I.T. DURING THE WAR...

... FLYING DANGEROUS MISSIONS OVER THE CHARLES RIVER...

*No, not what they were actually called.

SO WHILE YOUR AVERAGE CITIZEN OF CLEVELAND HAS BARELY EVEN **SEEN** A PLANE FLY OVER OUR FAIR CITY...

.... OUR CENTERFIELDER'S GOT HIS PILOT'S LICENSE AND BELONGS TO A LOCAL AVIATION CLUB.

OH YES -- AND THEN THERE'S HIS BASEBALL CAREER.
SPOKE PLAYS CENTERFIELD SO SHALLOW THAT HE'S PRACTICALLY AN INFIELDER...
... BUT STILL MANAGES TO GRAB ALL THOSE LONG BALLS.

IN ADDITION TO INNOVATING ON THE BALLFIELD, HE'S PROVEN HIMSELF TO BE QUITE THE CUTTING-EDGE MANAGER. HE'S INVENTED THIS TACTIC CALLED "PLATOONING," THAT IS, BATTING HIS LEFTIES AGAINST OPPOSING RIGHT-HANDED PITCHERS (AND VICE-VERSA) WITH THE IDEA THEY CAN HIT THEM BETTER.

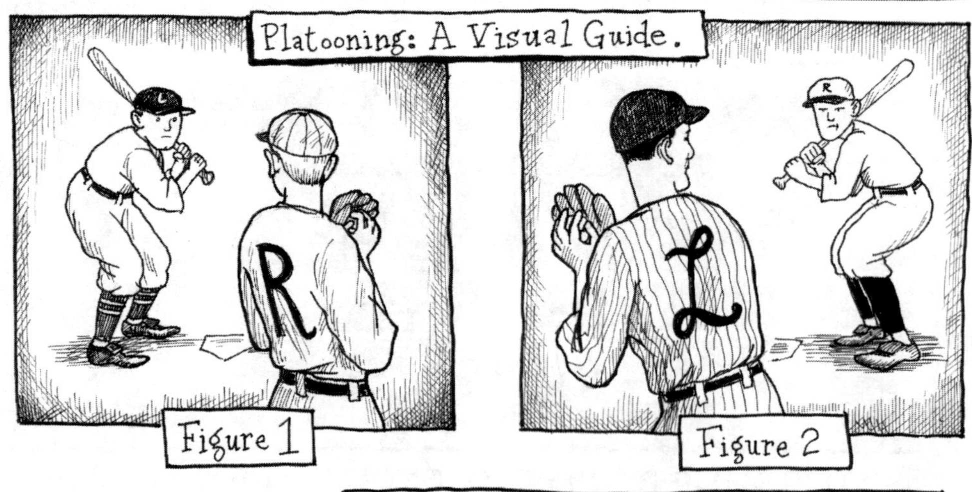

(WE'LL SEE IF IT TAKES OFF)

AFTER LEADING THE BOSTON RED SOX TO WORLD SERIES VICTORIES IN 1912 AND 1915, HE WAS TRADED TO THE INDIANS. WE'RE HOPING SOME OF HIS MAGIC RUBS OFF ON **OUR CLUB**!

SURE, HE TOOK A LITTLE WHILE TO WARM UP TO THE IDEA OF COMING HERE...

PLAY FOR... CLEVELAND?
A SEVENTH-PLACE TEAM?
NOW, WHY THE HELL WOULD I WANT TO DO THAT?
·1916·

OKAY, HE DIDN'T REALLY HAVE A CHOICE. MUCH TO HIS SURPRISE, HOWEVER, HE'S COME TO LOVE IT HERE. FOR ONE THING, HE'S BECOME ALMOST IMMEDIATE BUDDIES WITH OUR SHORTSTOP, RAY CHAPMAN.

WHY, CHAPPIE AND SPOKE ARE LIKE **BROTHERS**!

THEY ROOMED TOGETHER UNTIL RECENTLY, WHEN CHAPPIE GOT MARRIED. MR. SPEAKER SAYS HE'S QUITE FOND OF HIS BEST FRIEND'S **NEW MISSUS**...

... AND SEEMS TO LIKE **HER COUSIN JANE** JUST FINE, TOO.

WHILE THEY'VE NOW SETTLED HERE IN THE MIDWEST, THESE TWO ARE STILL **SOUTHERN BOYS** AT HEART...

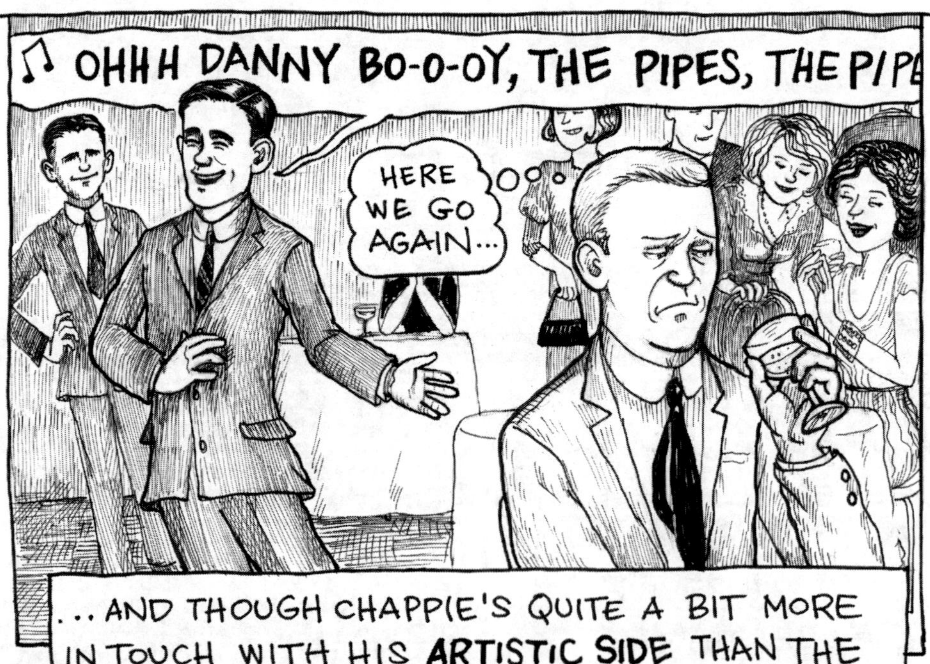

♫ OHHH DANNY BO-O-OY, THE PIPES, THE PIPE
HERE WE GO AGAIN...

... AND THOUGH CHAPPIE'S QUITE A BIT MORE IN TOUCH WITH HIS **ARTISTIC SIDE** THAN THE RUGGED SPOKE, IT'S A SURE BET THAT THIS PAIR IS BOUND TO BE **PALS FOR LIFE**.

10

Spoke & Slim

(or, Kicking the Sauce ... the Tris Speaker Way.)

The Cleveland Indians acquired knuckleballer Raymond "Slim" Caldwell toward the end of the 1919 season.

HE'S SIZZLING!
UM... SHOULD WE EVEN TOUCH HIM?

I'M OKAY...
I THINK.

SLIM WAS STRUCK BY LIGHTNING IN HIS FIRST APPEARANCE IN CLEVELAND'S LEAGUE PARK--MOST FOLKS WOULD CALL THAT AN INAUSPICIOUS START. INCREDIBLY, HE FINISHED AND **WON** THAT GAME. BUT THE INDIANS HAD SOMETHING MORE FORMIDABLE THAN AN ACT OF GOD TO CONTEND WITH IN ORDER TO KEEP SLIM ALIVE AND IN THE PITCHING ROTATION: HIS **BOOZING**.

SLIM'S PRODIGIOUS DRINKING WAS HARDLY NEW. HE HAD BEEN IN BASEBALL FOR NINE YEARS, ALSO VEXING MANAGERS OF HIS PREVIOUS TEAMS: THE YANKEES AND RED SOX.

AND NOW, AS IF HE DIDN'T HAVE **ENOUGH** TO DO, NEWLY JUGGLING HIS DUTIES AS STAR CENTERFIELDER AND MANAGER, TRIS SPEAKER WAS FACED WITH AN AGE-OLD CHALLENGE: HOW DO YOU GET A DRUNK NOT TO DRINK? SPECIFICALLY... WHEN YOU NEED HIM TO **PITCH**?

THE ANSWER, SPOKE DECIDED, WOULD HAVE TO LIE IN THE CONTRACT.

THERE!

SO, WHERE'S A FELLA GOT TO GO TO GET A DRINK IN CLEVELAND?
SLIM-
MAKE SURE YOU READ YOUR CONTRACT.

WHAT THE...
HEH HEH

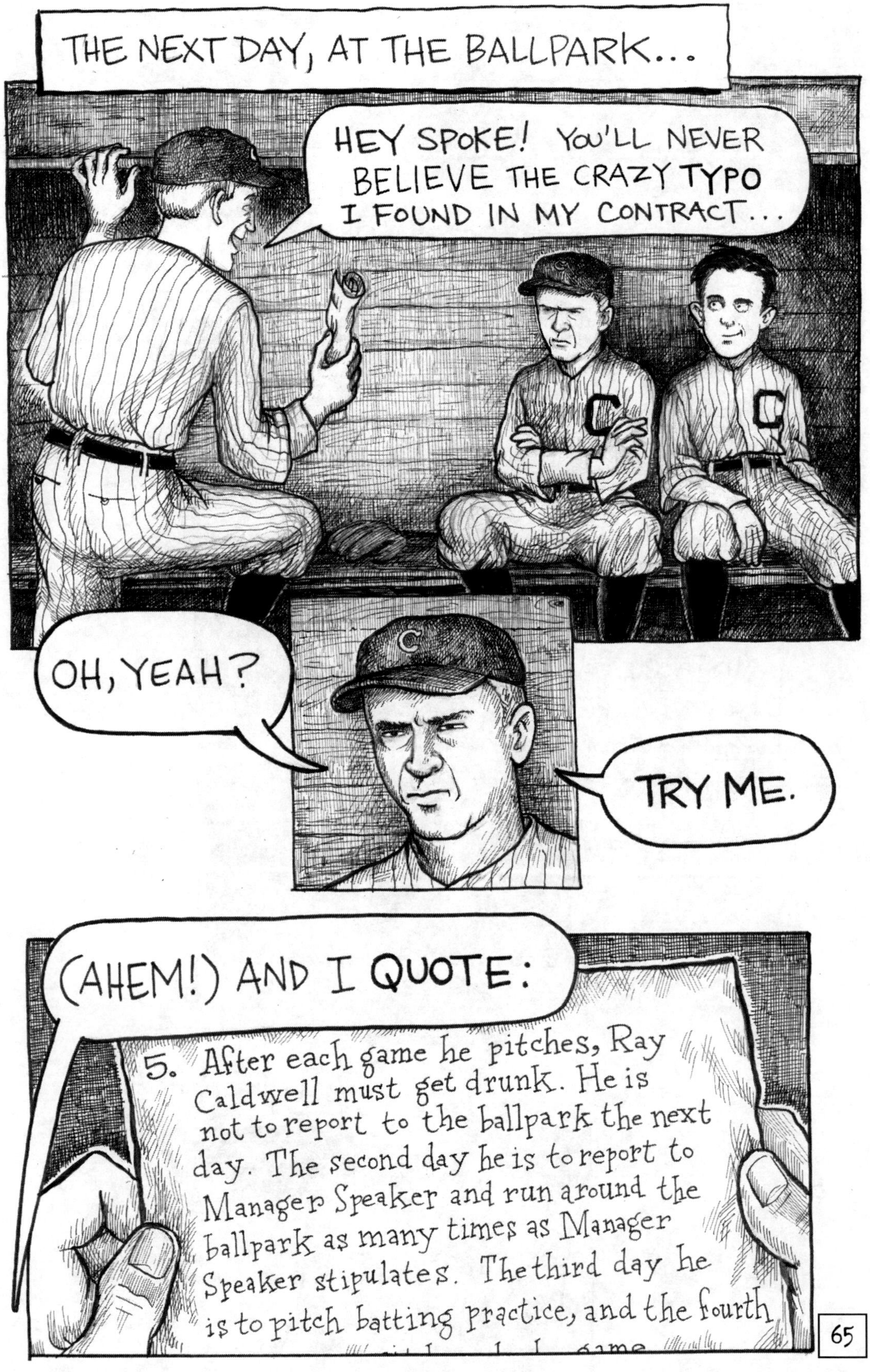

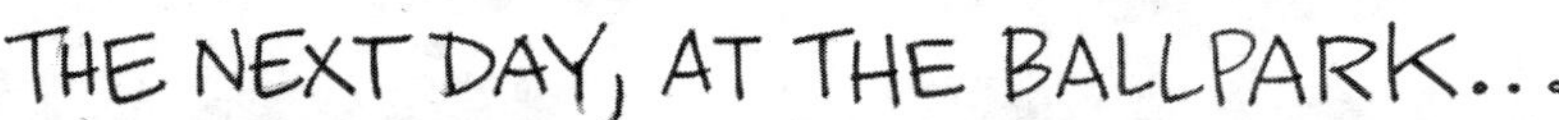

HEY SPOKE! YOU'LL NEVER BELIEVE THE CRAZY TYPO I FOUND IN MY CONTRACT...

OH, YEAH?

TRY ME.

(AHEM!) AND I QUOTE:

5. After each game he pitches, Ray Caldwell must get drunk. He is not to report to the ballpark the next day. The second day he is to report to Manager Speaker and run around the ballpark as many times as Manager Speaker stipulates. The third day he is to pitch batting practice, and the fourth

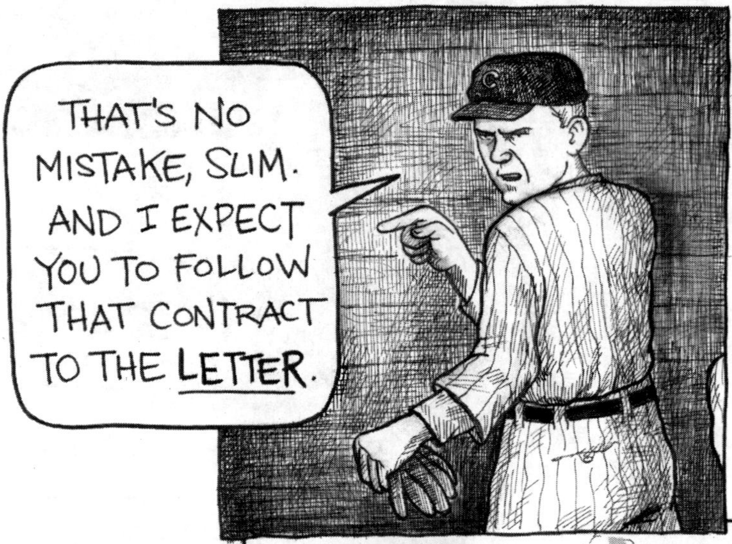

THAT'S NO MISTAKE, SLIM. AND I EXPECT YOU TO FOLLOW THAT CONTRACT TO THE LETTER.

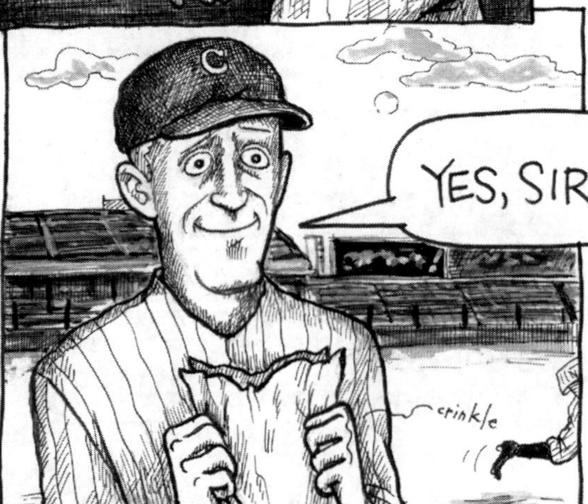

YES, SIR!

crinkle

THUS BEGAN SLIM'S ROTATION, AS SCHEDULED:

DAY • ONE

NICE GAME TODAY, SLIM!

GLUG!

Pitch, Then Get Drunk

DAY • TWO

IT'S IN HIS CONTRACT, YOU KNOW.

WHAT?!

DON'T COME TO BALLPARK.

DAY • THREE

JUST FIVE MORE.

RUN (ENDLESS) LAPS

DAY • FOUR

PITCH BATTING PRACTICE

SPEAKER'S PLAN WORKED. SLIM TURNED OUT TO BE AN **EFFECTIVE** (THAT IS, SOBER AND NOT VISIBLY HUNG OVER) **ADDITION** TO HIS PITCHING STAFF.

NOT ONLY THAT, BUT SOMEWHERE ALONG THE WAY, SLIM BEGAN TO LOSE HIS TASTE FOR THE HARD STUFF. GETTING DRUNK JUST WASN'T AS APPEALING WHEN IT WAS, WELL, **REQUIRED**. AS ONE CLEVELAND SPORTSWRITER PUT IT...

"IT WAS SUSPECTED THAT HE SOMETIMES VIOLATED THE AGREEMENT BY GOING HOME AND CURLING UP WITH A GOOD BOOK." HIS CAREER-HIGH TWENTY WINS IN 1920 HELPED MAKE THAT CHAMPIONSHIP SEASON POSSIBLE.

(NOTE SUBTLE 1921 UNIFORMS)

HE BID SPOKE (AND BASEBALL) **FAREWELL** IN 1921, THAT IS, UNTIL A CHANCE ENCOUNTER MANY YEARS LATER...

NEW YORK STATE, 1948:
TRIS SPEAKER WALKS INTO A BAR...
SLIM?!
huh?

SPOKE!

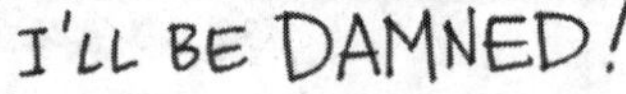
I'LL BE DAMNED!

SO... YOU TENDING BAR?
I CAN'T SAY IT'S THE BEST IDEA I EVER HEARD...

OH, I HAVEN'T HAD A DRINK IN YEARS! A GLASS OF BEER NOW AND THEN, BUT NO WHISKEY.
THAT CONTRACT YOU WROTE DONE CURED ME!

11 RAY CHAPMAN'S LAST GAME

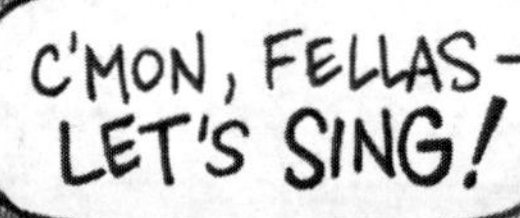

WELCOME TO THE POLO GROUNDS, HOME OF THE NEW YORK YANKEES!
... AND THE GIANTS, TOO, BUT THEY'RE ON THE ROAD RIGHT NOW.

SEE, THE CLEVELAND CLUB IS BASICALLY TIED WITH CHICAGO...

A Yankees Fan & His Lady
.. AND THE YANKEES ARE NIPPING AT THEIR HEELS IN THE STANDINGS...
...SO THIS IS A BIG GAME!

OH, REALLY?
YAAWWN

AND THERE'S MAYS, OUR STARTER, WARMING UP.
CHECK OUT THAT DELIVERY!
YUCK! HE LOOKS CRAZY!

IT AIN'T PRETTY, BUT IT WORKS! CHAPPIE- THAT'S CLEVELAND'S SHORTSTOP-SAYS, "I CAN'T HIT HIM, BUT THE OTHER BOYS..."
"CHAPPIE"? IS THAT RAY CHAPMAN?

SAY, YOU'RE GETTING THE HANG OF THIS AFTER ALL!

OH, I'VE SEEN HIS PICTURE...
HE SURE IS DREAMY!

AT THE TOP OF THE FIFTH INNING, THE SCORE STANDS AT 3 TO NOTHING IN CLEVELAND'S FAVOR.

CARL MAYS' WIFE IS AT THE GAME, HOPING TO WITNESS HER HUSBAND'S 100TH WIN.

RAY CHAPMAN APPROACHES THE PLATE. SO FAR IN THE GAME HE'S BEEN O-FOR-1 WITH A SACRIFICE BUNT, AND IS LEADING THE LEAGUE IN SACRIFICE HITS YET AGAIN. SPEAKER WAITS ON DECK.

WHILE DELIVERING HIS FIRST PITCH TO CHAPMAN, MAYS SEES HIS FOOT MOVE– A SIGN HE'S PLANNING ANOTHER BUNT.

HE RESPONDS BY SENDING THE PITCH UP AND IN.

LATER, WHILE MAKING HIS OFFICIAL STATEMENT TO THE MANHATTAN DISTRICT ATTORNEY, MAYS WOULD RECALL THAT CHAPMAN **DUCKED** AS THE BALL APPROACHED.

ACCORDING TO EVERY OTHER EYEWITNESS...

... HE **NEVER MOVED A MUSCLE**.

CATCHER MUDDY RUEL COULD SEE EXACTLY WHERE THE PITCH WAS HEADED: ON THE INSIDE, BUT WITHIN THE STRIKE ZONE.

CHAPMAN SEEMED HYPNOTIZED BY THE BALL HEADING TOWARDS HIM.

"WHY DIDN'T HE REACT, DUCK, THROW HIMSELF ON THE GROUND?" ASKED SPORTSWRITER FRED LIEB, WHO WATCHED FROM THE PRESS BOX BEHIND HOME PLATE.

WHEN THE BALL HIT CHAPMAN'S LEFT TEMPLE, THE LOUD CRACK WAS HEARD THROUGHOUT THE BALLPARK, BUT FEW PRESENT REALIZED WHAT THAT SOUND ACTUALLY MEANT.

WHAT WAS THAT?

CLEVELAND COACH JACK McCALLISTER HEARD "AN EXPLOSIVE SOUND"

MOST OF THE PLAYERS ON THE FIELD ASSUMED THIS SOUND WAS THE BALL HITTING HIS BAT, INCLUDING MAYS AND FIRST BASEMAN WALLY PIPP, WHO ROUTINELY FIELDED THE BALL THAT HAD JUST RICHOCHETED OFF CHAPMAN'S SKULL.

CHAPMAN REMAINED MOTIONLESS FOR A BRIEF MOMENT, THEN BEGAN TO CRUMPLE TO THE GROUND. RUEL TRIED—BUT FAILED—TO CATCH HIM.

IT WOULD HAUNT HIM FOR THE REST OF HIS LIFE.

ONCE IT WAS CLEAR HE WAS HURT, THOSE WHO RUSHED TO HIS AID FOUND A MACABRE SCENE.

GOOD GOD!

FRED LIEB CLAIMED THAT CHAPMAN'S LEFT EYE WAS HANGING FROM ITS SOCKET.

HE STARTED TO REGAIN CONSCIOUSNESS . . .

...AT WHICH POINT, ACCORDING TO SPEAKER, HE ATTEMPTED TO GET UP AND CHARGE AT MAYS.

ONLY ONE PLAYER REMAINED IN THE CLEVELAND DUGOUT.

"I HEARD THE SOUND WHEN IT HIT HIM," THIRD BASEMAN LARRY GARDNER SAID. "I DIDN'T NEED A CLOSER VIEW."

ALL THIS TIME, THE MAJORITY OF THE FANS WERE CLUELESS.

IS HE GETTING UP?
HE JUST NEEDS TO GET THAT NOGGIN ICED!

THE GAME RESUMED, AND HE WAS ESCORTED BACK TO THE CLUBHOUSE. HIS CONDITION **DETERIORATED SWIFTLY**. IT WAS EVIDENT HE WAS IN **SERIOUS TROUBLE**.

WHILE THE TEAM'S TRAINER ICED HIS HEAD, CHAPPIE SPOKE URGENTLY AND INCOHERENTLY.

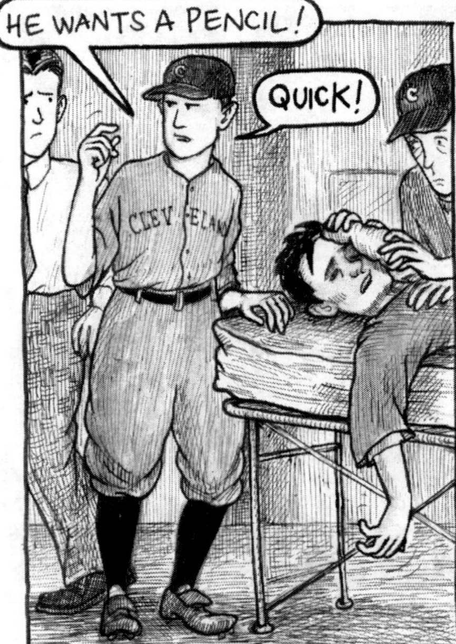

HE WANTS A PENCIL!
QUICK!
CLEVELAN

TAKE YOUR TIME...

...BUT HE WAS TOO DAZED TO WRITE ANYTHING.

HE GOT OUT A DEMAND FOR "KATY'S RING" TO THE TRAINER, WHO OFTEN HELD IT FOR HIM DURING BALLGAMES...

... AND VISIBLY RELAXED ONCE IT WAS BACK ON HIS FINGER.

WHEN THE AMBULANCE FINALLY ARRIVED, CHAPPIE SAID TO HIS FRIEND JOHN HENRY...

PROMISE ME...

WHATEVER YOU DO, DON'T CALL KATY. BUT IF YOU DO... TELL HER I'M ALL RIGHT.

12

The Yankees' WALLY PIPP in: The View from First.

IT WAS THE VERY FIRST PITCH OF THE FIFTH INNING.

IT COULD HAVE BEEN A BUNT. IT ACTED LIKE ONE. SOUNDED LIKE ONE. CHAPMAN BUNTED A FAIR AMOUNT. RIGHTLY SO, HE WAS SO DARNED **FAST**. CARL WAS EXPECTING ONE TOO, AND HE SCOOPED IT RIGHT UP.

A ROUTINE PLAY. HE THREW IT TO ME, I STEPPED ON THE BAG, TURNED TO TOSS THE BALL AROUND THE BASES... LIKE HUNDREDS OF TIMES BEFORE.

THEN I SAW HIM.

C
LEVEL

HE HIT THE GROUND, AND WITHIN MOMENTS WAS SURROUNDED.

I DON'T THINK CARL REALIZED WHAT HE'D DONE UNTIL HE SAW MY REACTION.

AT WHICH POINT HE DID... **NOTHING.**
HE REMAINED ON THE MOUND, EXPRESSIONLESS.

HE **HAD** TO BE IN SHOCK.

AT LEAST, I **HOPE** HE WAS.
I ADMIT THAT I WAS, AT FIRST.

ANYWAY, IT'S THE ONLY EXPLANATION I CAN THINK OF FOR WHAT CARL DID NEXT.

I SNAPPED TO ATTENTION. HE WAS RAISING A RUCKUS WITH UMPIRE CONNOLLY, MAKING WILD CLAIMS THAT THE BALL HAD HIT CHAPMAN'S BAT, NOT HIS HEAD: THAT HE WAS... **FAKING**.

I INTERVENED, TRYING TO CALM HIM DOWN BEFORE HE DID ANY MORE DAMAGE. THE BOYS FROM THE CLEVELAND CLUB WERE LIABLE TO COME AFTER HIM IF HE PUSHED THIS MUCH FURTHER. NOT THAT I'D REALLY BLAME THEM.

THE BALL? ONLY THEN DID I REALIZE I WAS STILL CLUTCHING IT IN MY HAND. I GAVE IT TO HIM AND REGRETTED IT ALMOST INSTANTLY.

OH, BROTHER.
SEE THESE **SCRATCHES**? THAT'S WHAT MADE THE BALL VEER INSIDE LIKE THAT. IT'S IN **TERRIBLE** CONDITION!

I FELT SOME RELIEF THAT HE WAS FINALLY **ADMITTING** HE HIT THE POOR FELLOW... BUT CARL'S JUSTIFICATIONS WERE HARDLY HELPING HIS CASE. IN FACT, QUITE THE CONTRARY.

MEANWHILE, A COUPLE OF CHAPMAN'S TEAMMATES WERE HELPING HIM OFF THE FIELD. HE WALKED ON HIS OWN FOR A BIT...

... BUT SOON COLLAPSED AGAIN. THEY HAD TO CARRY HIM THE REST OF THE WAY. I GOT A REALLY SICK FEELING THEN. I'D NEVER SEEN A MAN IN SUCH BAD SHAPE ON THE DIAMOND -- AND HAVEN'T SINCE.

OF COURSE, THERE WAS A GAME TO FINISH. BASEBALL'S RHYTHM LULLED US ALL BACK TO THE ROUTINE.

A PINCH RUNNER APPEARED AT FIRST...

SPEAKER WAS UP AT BAT...

AND SO THE GAME WENT ON. WE ALL TOLD OURSELVES THAT CHAPMAN WAS PROBABLY GOING TO BE ALL RIGHT. WERE WE IN DENIAL? MAYBE. BUT WE HAD TO KEEP PLAYING.

CARL STAYED IN THE GAME AFTER THE BEANING. HE PLAYED THROUGH THE EIGHTH INNING, IN FACT.

AS FAR AS HIS PITCHING WENT, HE SEEMED... UNAFFECTED.

WE ENDED UP LOSING THE GAME. SEEMS LIKE A FUNNY THING TO MENTION IN LIGHT OF WHAT HAPPENED. BUT THAT'S WHY WE WERE ALL THERE, RIGHT? ANYWAY, YOU CAN CHECK OUT THE BOX SCORE IF YOU WANT TO KNOW ANY MORE.

THAT GAME WAS ONE I'LL PROBABLY NEVER FORGET, NO MATTER HOW HARD I TRY.

DO I THINK THAT CARL MAYS HIT RAY CHAPMAN ON **PURPOSE**? OF COURSE NOT.

BUT THINKING BACK ON HIS STRANGE BEHAVIOR THAT DAY, I CAN SEE HOW SOMEONE ELSE MIGHT.

13

Post-Game, Yankees Clubhouse

WOULD YOU LIKE TO TALK ABOUT WHAT HAPPENED DURING THE GAME TODAY?

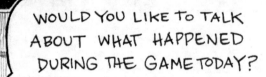

F.C. Lane, editor & writer for "Baseball Magazine"

NOT REALLY.

YOU SURE?
Exit
HOW THINGS LOOKED FROM YOUR POINT OF VIEW?

FINE.
COME ON OVER.

I WAS **WILD** AS A **HAWK** TODAY...
I ALWAYS AM WHEN I'M SAVED UP FOR A BIG GAME.

HUGGINS KNOWS THAT...
..BUT WHEN YOUR TEAM SAYS PITCH, YOU PITCH.

MAYS

AND THE BALL...
IT WAS WET. REALLY SLIPPERY

IS HE... BADLY HURT?
HAVE YOU SEEN HIM?

MAYS
(AHEM)
I HAVEN'T.

CARL...
AN AMBULANCE TOOK HIM AWAY JUST A FEW MINUTES AGO.

Exi

MAYS!

WE SHOULD GO DOWN TO THE POLICE STATION. THEY'RE GOING TO WANT A STATEMENT FROM YOU.

DAMMIT, CARL...
I JUST THINK IT'D BE A GOOD IDEA.

I'LL WAIT FOR YOU BY YOUR CAR.

NEW YORK, AUGUST 17, 10 a.m.

14

Upon receiving word of her husband's injury, Katy Chapman took the overnight train from Cleveland to New York City.

TRIS...

HE'S DEAD, ISN'T HE?

KATY...

The New York Times, August 18, 1920

RAY CHAPMAN DIES; MAYS EXONERATED.

Widow Takes Body of Ball-Player, Killed by Pitched Ball, Back to Cleveland.

Pitcher Who Threw Ball Unnerved by Accident — Other Teams Would Bar Him.

MIDNIGHT OPERATION FAILS

Player's Brain Crushed by Force of Blow — District Attorney Says Accident Was Unavoidable.

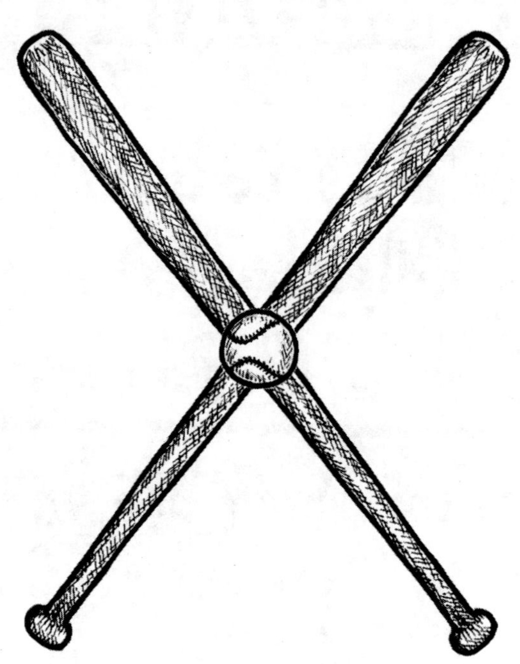

Part III

Aftermath.

The Mays Residence.

Early morning, Tuesday August 17.

YOU WORK FOR THE BALLCLUB, DON'T YOU?
I'VE GOT SOME BAD NEWS FOR YOU.

RAY CHAPMAN... DIED AT FIVE O'CLOCK THIS MORNING.

MAYS THE MURDERER

THE NEWS OF CHAPMAN'S DEATH SEND SHOCKWAVES THROUGHOUT BASEBALL. BUT IT DIDN'T TAKE LONG FOR DEMANDS THAT MAYS BE HELD ACCOUNTABLE TO DROWN OUT THE MOURNING. THERE WAS NO WAY TO BRING CHAPPIE BACK...

I... CAN'T BELIEVE HE'S... GONE!
SHHH...
CHAPPIE...
OF ALL PEOPLE...

WAIT A MINUTE!

THAT BASTARD MAYS IS GONNA PAY!

... BUT THERE WAS DEFINITELY SOMEONE TO BLAME.

UNSURPRISINGLY, CHAPPIE'S TEAMMATES WERE QUICK TO PUBLICLY CONDEMN THE MAN WHO THREW THE FATAL PITCH.

HE OUGHTA BE STRUNG UP!
DOC JOHNSTON, INDIANS' FIRST BASEMAN

Poll of Cleveland Players UNANIMOUS: MAYS DELIBERATELY FIRED AT CHAPMAN'S HEAD!

AND MEMBERS OF THE PRESS WEREN'T SHY ABOUT VILIFYING MAYS, EITHER . . .

CARL MAYS · MUST · GO!

A Menace to the Welfare of Baseball!

PLAYERS HATE & FEAR HIM!

BY AUGUST 24, A WEEK AFTER CHAPPIE'S DEATH, THE CLEVELAND BOYS MADE AN UNPRECENTED MOVE. THEY DREW UP A PETITION STATING THAT THEY WOULD REFUSE TO PARTICIPATE IN ANY GAME IN WHICH CARL MAYS WAS PLAYING...

WE, THE UNDERSIGNED, members of the Cleveland
se Ball Club, have resolved to take no part in any ball
e in which Mr Carl Mays shall take part.

EVERY PLAYER ON THE TEAM SIGNED IT...

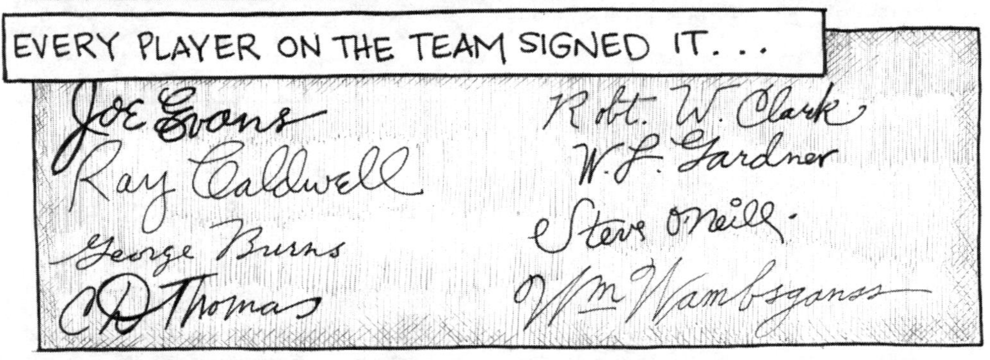

... EXCEPT FOR **ONE**.

BANG BANG

SPOKE?!

SPOKE?

HEY, OPEN UP! WE'VE GOT A PETITION FOR YOU TO SIGN.

HMM..

WE'RE GONNA **GET** THAT HEADHUNTER FOR WHAT HE DID!

HE MUST BE ASLEEP.

DESPITE THE PROFOUND EFFECT CHAPMAN'S DEATH HAD ON HIM, AND HIS PERSONAL DISLIKE OF MAYS (DATING BACK TO THEIR YEAR TOGETHER ON THE RED SOX)...

... SPEAKER WAS MORE MEASURED THAN ONE MIGHT EXPECT WHEN HE WAS TOLD OF THE GROWING MOVEMENT TO BAN MAYS FROM BASEBALL.

I'M ALL BROKEN UP...
I CAN'T DO ANYTHING RIGHT NOW, BUT I'M CONVINCED IT WAS AN ACCIDENT.

BOYCOTT MAYS? WITH PLEASURE!
GIMME THAT!
ME NEXT!

MAYS' **OTHER** FORMER TEAMMATES WEREN'T NEARLY SO KIND. WHILE THEY STILL RESENTED HIM FOR ABANDONING THE SOX THE YEAR BEFORE, THEY ALSO KNEW HIM — AND HIS METHODS — BETTER THAN **ANYONE**. AS A RESULT, THEY WERE QUICK TO JOIN CLEVELAND ON THE BOYCOTT BANDWAGON.

EVEN TEAMS WITHOUT MAYS BAGGAGE HAD SOME POINTED WORDS TO SAY. THE ST. LOUIS BROWNS SEEMED TO HAVE SEEN IT COMING:

"If the news had come over the wire that a ball player had been killed by a pitched ball, the Browns to a man would have guessed **who did the pitching.**"

ALL TOLD, THREE TEAMS SIGNED THE PETITION AND BELIEVED MAYS' ACT TO BE INTENTIONAL.

BY THE TIME A.L. PRESIDENT BAN JOHNSON RECEIVED A COPY OF THE PETITION, THE BOYCOTT THREAT HAD SNOWBALLED. TWO OTHER TEAMS PROMISED TO JOIN IN ONCE IT WENT INTO EFFECT. HE HAD TO ACT.

SIR... LOOKS LIKE THREE BALL CLUBS ARE REFUSING TO PLAY WITH MAYS...
MAYS AGAIN.... THAT MAN IS THE BANE OF MY EXISTENCE!

JOHNSON WAS NO FAN OF MAYS DUE TO HIS ANTICS WITH THE RED SOX THE SEASON BEFORE, BUT ALLOWING THE PLAYERS TO SEIZE POWER LIKE THIS WOULD SET A DANGEROUS PRECEDENT. HE ORDERED THAT ANY TEAM THAT TOOK PART WOULD FACE DIRE CONSEQUENCES: FINES AND FORFEITED GAMES.

MEANWHILE, MAYS' BEHAVIOR IN THE DAYS FOLLOWING CHAPMAN'S DEATH WAS REGARDED WITH SOME SUSPICION.

HE NEVER EVEN TRIED TO CONTACT CHAPPIE'S WIDOW TO OFFER HIS CONDOLENCES OR APOLOGIZE!

HIS FELLOW PLAYERS DECRIED MAYS' TECHNIQUES WITH A FRESH, RETROACTIVE OUTRAGE:

IT'S A **MIRACLE** THIS HADN'T HAPPENED SOONER. HE'S ALWAYS BEEN A **HEADHUNTER**!

HE'S A **FREAK** PITCHER WITH AN **UNNATURAL** DELIVERY...

EVEN HIS **CATCHERS** HAVE SAID SO!

WHEN MAYS PITCHES OVERHAND, IT'S LIKELY TO GO ANYPLACE.

WALLY SCHANG

I DON'T KNOW HOW I EVER CAUGHT ANY OF THEM.
MUDDY RUEL

AN INSCRUTABLE PITCHER WITH A PENCHANT FOR THROWING DANGEROUSLY INSIDE... AND YET, MAYS WAS EFFECTIVE, ONE OF THE LEAGUE'S BEST. HE HAD CONTROL, ALL RIGHT... **WHEN IT SUITED HIM**.

IN THE MIDST OF THE CONTROVERSY CAME HIS FIRST INTERVIEW SINCE THE INCIDENT. RUMORS THAT MAYS WAS IN SECLUSION, DISTRAUGHT AND INCONSOLABLE, PROVED GREATLY EXAGGERATED, ACCORDING TO THE REPORTERS THAT SPOKE WITH HIM IN HIS LIVING ROOM DAYS AFTER CHAPMAN'S DEATH.

MY CONSCIENCE IS ABSOLUTELY CLEAR.
IF IT WEREN'T, I COULD NEVER THINK OF GOING NEAR A BALLPARK AGAIN.
I AM ABSOLUTELY **BLAMELESS.**

AND AS HE HELD HIS INFANT DAUGHTER, MAYS FED THE FIRE OF SCANDAL FURTHER.

IT WAS THE UMPIRE'S FAULT.
THEY'RE SUPPOSED TO REPLACE BALLS THAT ARE ROUGHED UP.

ISN'T SHE CUTE?

THUS HE HAD A NEW SET OF ENEMIES CALLING FOR HIS HEAD.

HIS FELLOW UMPIRES JUMPED TO HIS DEFENSE, HURLING THE BLAME BACK AT HIS ACCUSER, STATING THAT "NO PITCHER IN THE AMERICAN LEAGUE RESORTED TO TRICKERY MORE."

UNTIL THE NEW PITCHING RULES CAME INTO FORCE* MAYS USED TO CONSTANTLY RUB THE BALL ACROSS THE PITCHING RUBBER TO ROUGHEN THE SURFACE.
YEAH.
BILLY EVANS AND BILL DINNEEN, IN CRISIS MODE

MAYS HAD A SLOW START THAT YEAR, AND THERE HAD ALREADY BEEN SUPPOSITIONS THAT HE RELIED SO HEAVILY ON THE OUTLAWED "TRICK PITCHES", HE NEEDED AMPLE EXTRA TIME TO FIGURE OUT HOW TO PITCH CLEAN.

THE UMPS, FURTHER SEEKING TO EXONERATE THEIR COLLEAGUE (AND THEMSELVES BY ASSOCIATION) WERE QUICK TO REMIND EVERYONE OF THE RECENT ORDER THAT THEY KEEP EACH BALL IN THE GAME FOR AS LONG AS POSSIBLE, AS TO DO OTHERWISE WOULD BE A FLAGRANT WASTE.

* AT THE START OF THE 1920 SEASON

WHEN MAYS FINALLY REJOINED HIS TEAM, IT WAS FOR A SERIES AGAINST THE DETROIT TIGERS IN NEW YORK. WITH THE TIGERS, OF COURSE, CAME BASEBALL'S PREMIER SOCIOPATH, TY COBB.

IF THERE WAS ONE PLAYER MORE PERSONALLY DISLIKED THAN CARL MAYS, IT WAS COBB. AND ALTHOUGH COBB HAD DONE MANY QUESTIONABLE THINGS...

HE'S GOT NO HANDS, MAN!

HA!

YOU OKAY?
whimper..

... AT LEAST HE HAD NEVER KILLED ANYONE. ON THE FIELD, ANYWAY.

THE TWO WERE HARDLY STRANGERS. THEY FIRST BUTTED HEADS IN 1915 WHEN MAYS THREW TOO CLOSE TO COBB'S HEAD FOR HIS LIKING...

COBB LIVED FOR GRUDGES. A COUPLE OF YEARS LATER MAYS BRUSHED HIM BACK AGAIN. AFTER FLINGING THE BAT AT HIM, HE BUNTED THE NEXT PITCH SO MAYS WOULD BE FORCED TO COVER FIRST...

...AND MAYS GOT THE COBB SPECIAL.

MAYS WAS SCARRED FOR LIFE.
PHYSICALLY, THAT IS.
HE STILL CLAIMED HE WASN'T AFRAID OF THE GEORGIA PEACH.

MEMBERS OF THE PRESS, AWARE OF THEIR BLOODY HISTORY AND MUTUAL DISLIKE, FIGURED IT WAS A SAFE BET TO REPEATEDLY QUOTE COBB AS CALLING FOR RETALIATION AGAINST MAYS...

"That Mays has been pitching like that since he came into the league. He killed a great little guy and a wonderful ballplayer. Give the man a taste of his own medicine, I say."

ACCORDING TO COBB, THESE QUOTES HAD BEEN FABRICATED, AND THIS ENRAGED HIM. HE HATED MAYS, CERTAINLY, BUT WASN'T INVOLVED IN THIS PARTICULAR FIGHT--YET.

WHEN THE SERIES BEGAN, THOUGH HE WAS SICK WITH THE FLU, COBB ABSOLUTELY INSISTED ON PLAYING...

GET OFFA ME!
BUT, SIR... YOU'RE VERY ILL...

... BECAUSE HE REFUSED TO LET THE NEW YORK FANS (THE ONLY PEOPLE ON EARTH DEFENDING CARL MAYS FROM ALL THE HOSTILITY DIRECTED HIS WAY)--

I CAN'T BELIEVE WHAT HE'S SAYING ABOUT POOR MAYS!
I MEAN, OL' CARL'S A WEIRDO..
...BUT IT WAS OBVIOUSLY AN ACCIDENT!

-- THINK THAT HE WAS AFRAID TO FACE THEM.

AND SO, ON MAYS' FIRST GAME BACK IN A YANKEES UNIFORM, THE FEVERISH COBB FACED DOWN THE ANGRY MOB WITH HIS PATENTED BRAND OF DEMENTED PANACHE.

A COUPLE OF DAYS LATER, MAYS WAS FINALLY SET TO MAKE HIS RETURN TO THE MOUND. SHORTLY BEFORE THE GAME BEGAN, A BAT BOY APPROACHED HIM.

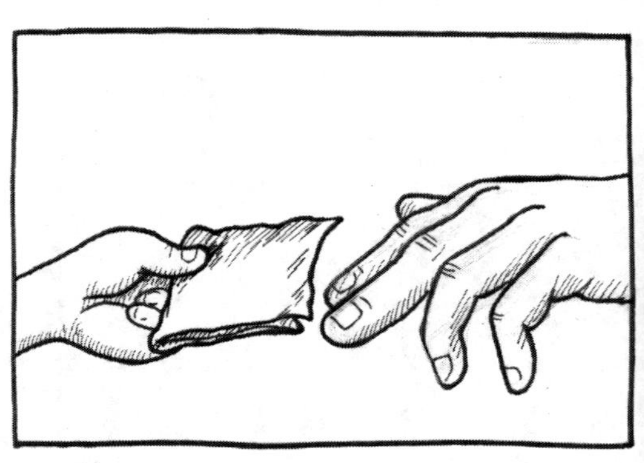

If it was within my power I would have inscribed on Chapman's tombstone these words:
"HERE LIES THE VICTIM OF ARROGANCE, VICIOUSNESS and GREED."

TY COBB GAVE THIS TO YOU?
ARE YOU SURE?

YEP.
IT WAS HIM, ALL RIGHT.

OKAY, THANKS.
RUN ALONG.

DESPITE HIS PART IN CHAPMAN'S DEATH, AND HAVING ENDURED WHAT WAS SURELY A RATTLING MOMENT JUST BEFORE THE GAME'S START, MAYS SHUT OUT THE TIGERS THAT DAY.

WAS THIS FURTHER PROOF THAT MAYS WAS A MONSTER? ANYONE WHO COULD PERFORM SO WELL UNDER THESE CIRCUMSTANCES **HAD** TO BE, RIGHT?

EVEN WHEN HE WON, WELL... MAYS COULD NEVER WIN.

16

A Defense Of Carl Mays

I CANNOT PREVENT PEOPLE FROM DISLIKING ME, NOR CAN I BLAME THEM FOR DOING SO.

NEARLY EVERYTHING CARL MAYS DID, OR DIDN'T DO, OR INDEED HAD EVER DONE CAME UNDER SCRUTINY AFTER CHAPMAN'S DEATH.

FEW AMONG THE MASSES REELING AFTER THE DEATH OF THIS HEALTHY, WELL-LIKED TWENTY-NINE-YEAR-OLD ATHLETE WHO DIED PLAYING BASEBALL (OF ALL THINGS!) HAD THE INCLINATION TO STOP AND THINK ABOUT WHAT THE MAN WHO THREW THAT PITCH MIGHT BE GOING THROUGH.

W.O. MCGEEHAN WARNED MOURNERS THUSLY IN THE NEW YORK TRIBUNE:

It is unfortunate that Mays has not been as popular as the dead player, but he must not be sacrificed for his unpopularity.

BUT IT WAS TOO LATE. THE SACRIFICE WAS UNDERWAY.

MAYS WAS OFTEN DESCRIBED AS A **LONER**, BUT **"MISFIT"** IS REALLY MORE APT. HE'D NEVER MADE FRIENDS EASILY, AND WHEN HE CAME UP TO THE BIG LEAGUES, THAT DIDN'T CHANGE. "THERE WERE A LOT OF COLLEGE MEN ON THE RED SOX," HE RECALLED. "I WAS VERY SELF-CONSCIOUS ABOUT IT AND KEPT TO MYSELF... AND THERE WERE OTHERS WHO LIKED TO ROISTER ABOUT DURING THE NIGHT. SO THEY CALLED ME A LONER."

ACCORDING TO CARL, HE JUST **DIDN'T HAVE A PLACE** IN ANY OF WHAT HE PERCEIVED AS BASEBALL'S **"CLIQUES."**

THAT, COUPLED WITH HIS DEEP INSECURITY ABOUT HIS **BACKGROUND** AND **LACK OF EDUCATION** (WHICH LOTS OF PLAYERS SHARED—A FACT THAT HE WAS APPARENTLY BLIND TO) LED HIM TO **SHUT HIMSELF OFF** FROM HIS TEAMMATES EARLY ON.

SO MAYS WASN'T A **NERD** OR A **PARTIER**, BUT HE WAS A **JOCK**, AND PREFERRED TO LET HIS PLAYING SPEAK FOR ITSELF. BUT THAT WASN'T ENOUGH FOR SOME PEOPLE. IF YOU ACCIDENTALLY **KILL** A MAN, YOU'LL NEED SOME **FRIENDS**.

AMID THE AFTERSHOCKS OF CHAPMAN'S DEATH, THE POPULAR BELIEF WAS THAT MAYS ACTED SUSPICIOUSLY, EVEN CALLOUSLY. IN REALITY, HE ATTEMPTED TO DO THE RIGHT THING, SUGGESTING TO THE YANKEES' OWNERS THAT HE VISIT CHAPMAN'S WIDOW.

HE COULDN'T HAVE WANTED TO — WHO IN HIS PLACE WOULD? — BUT HE DID OFFER. ULTIMATELY, HE WAS ADVISED THAT IT WOULD BE TOO DIFFICULT FOR HER. "I WOULD HAVE DONE IT IF ANY GOOD WOULD HAVE COME OF IT," HE LATER CLAIMED.

HE DID WRITE KATY CHAPMAN A LETTER, THE CONTENTS OF WHICH WE CAN ONLY **SPECULATE**.

HE DIDN'T ATTEND THE WAKE OR FUNERAL, BUT REMEMBER: HE WAS PRACTICALLY A WANTED MAN AT THIS POINT, AND DEATH THREATS HAD BEEN MADE AGAINST HIM. ATTENDING WOULD HAVE BROUGHT ATTENTION TO MAYS AT AN EVENT MEANT TO HONOR CHAPMAN. HE HAD **SELFISH REASONS**, TOO, AND ADMITTED AS MUCH:

"I KNEW THAT THE SIGHT OF HIS SILENT FORM WOULD HAUNT ME AS LONG AS I LIVED."

OF COURSE, HE DIDN'T NEED TO SEE THE BODY FOR CHAPMAN TO HAUNT HIM FOR THE REST OF HIS LIFE.

BETWEEN HIS MOODINESS, HIS FRIENDLESSNESS, AND HIS NOT-UNFOUNDED REPUTATION AS A SCOWLING LONER, MAYS WAS ALREADY SET UP TO BE THE PERFECT VILLAIN BEFORE HE EVER THREW THAT PITCH TO CHAPMAN. BUT HOW WOULD HE EVER RECOVER? THIS WAS UNCHARTERED TERRITORY.

BAN JOHNSON RELEASED A STATEMENT IN THE DAYS AFTER THE INCIDENT SUGGESTING THAT HE "MAY NEVER BE TEMPERAMENTALLY CAPABLE OF PITCHING AGAIN." IT'S NOT SO HARD TO IMAGINE, BUT QUITTING WASN'T MAYS' STYLE.

IT'S HARD TO OVERSTATE JUST HOW MUCH **COURAGE** IT TOOK FOR HIM TO RETURN TO THE PITCHER'S MOUND. THE FACT THAT HE CAME BACK AS GOOD, IF NOT BETTER, THAN BEFORE WAS — LIKE HIM OR NOT — A TESTAMENT TO HIS FOCUS AS AN ATHLETE.

NOT THAT HE WASN'T SCARED. "IT WAS NO EASY TASK TO PICK UP MY WORK WHERE I LEFT OFF," HE ADMITTED. THUS IN HIS FIRST GAME BACK, WITH EACH PITCH THAT HEADED TOWARD THE BATTER, HE FOUND HIMSELF YELLING:

PITCHING WAS HIS **JOB**, AND HE JUMPED RIGHT BACK INTO THE ROTATION AS SOON AS THE YANKEES ASKED HIM TO. THERE'S SOMETHING **ADMIRABLE** ABOUT THAT.

TODAY, OF COURSE, HIS NAME IS INEXTRICABLY LINKED TO BASEBALL'S ONLY FATAL BEANING, BUT CHARGES OF HEADHUNTING WERE ALREADY DOGGING MAYS WELL BEFORE THIS INCIDENT.

DID HE DESERVE THIS REPUTATION?

WHAT AN HONOR!
SAY CHEESE, CARL!

[NOT AN ACTUAL AWARD. OBVIOUSLY.]

HE LED THE LEAGUE IN HIT BATSMEN JUST ONCE -- IN 1917, WITH 14.

THE CONSENSUS AROUND THE LEAGUE WASN'T SO MUCH THAT HE HIT A LOT OF BATTERS (HIS CAREER TOTAL WASN'T ESPECIALLY HIGH WHEN COMPARED TO THAT OF THE ALL-TIME RECORD HOLDER) BUT THAT WHEN HE DID HIT SOMEONE, IT WAS USUALLY IN THE HEAD.

Walter Johnson, 206.

WE'LL NEVER KNOW IF THIS WAS ACTUALLY THE CASE, SINCE THERE AREN'T ANY RECORDS FOR HOW MANY BEANBALLS A PITCHER THROWS. BUT AS ONE PLAYER PUT IT, WHEN ASKED TO PROVE THE CLAIM THAT MAYS WAS A "BEANER".

HE WOULDN'T HAVE SUCH A REPUTATION IF IT WEREN'T TRUE.

SO THE LOGIC IS A LITTLE CIRCULAR ON THIS PARTICULAR ISSUE. MAYS HIT MORE BATTERS THAN AVERAGE, BUT THIS COULD BE CHALKED UP TO HIS STYLE OF DELIVERY, AT LEAST IN PART. THE UNDERHANDED SUBMARINE PITCH WAS NOTORIOUSLY TOUGH FOR HITTERS TO TRACK.

EMPLOYMENT OF THE INSIDE, OR "BRUSHBACK," PITCH HAD (AND HAS) ITS PLACE IN THE GAME, AND MAYS WAS HARDLY THE ONLY ONE DOING IT. WHETHER USED TO INTIMIDATE, RECLAIM THE STRIKE ZONE, OR SIMPLY MAKE A PITCH HARDER TO HIT, PITCHING TIGHT WAS AN **ACCEPTED PRACTICE**.

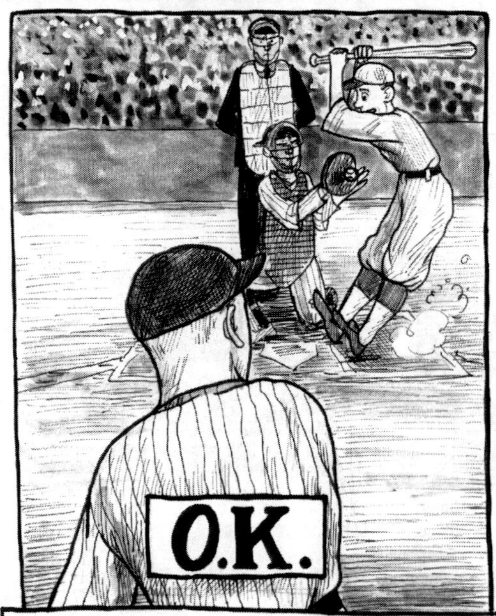

BEANING PLAYERS **PURPOSEFULLY**, HOWEVER, WAS NOT.

WHETHER TRUTH OR GROSS EXAGGERATION, MAYS USED THIS REPUTATION TO HIS ADVANTAGE. TY COBB ONCE ASKED HIM POINT-BLANK:

ARE YOU **TRYING** TO HIT ME?

IF YOU THINK I AM, **GREAT!**
JUST MAKES ME MORE EFFECTIVE.

THE STATEMENT MAY SEEM GHOULISH IN LIGHT OF WHAT WOULD HAPPEN LATER WITH CHAPMAN. REALLY, THOUGH, WASN'T HE JUST USING WHATEVER TOOLS HE HAD AT HIS DISPOSAL TO **WIN**?

AS TO THE CHARGES THAT HE "**DIDN'T CARE**" WHETHER HE HIT BATTERS?

AS PREVIOUSLY NOTED, WALTER JOHNSON HOLDS THE ALL-TIME RECORD FOR HIT BATSMEN, AND HE LED THE LEAGUE SEVERAL SEASONS.

HE WAS ALSO WIDELY CONSIDERED ONE OF THE GENTLEST MEN IN THE GAME, AND ALWAYS FEARED THAT HE'D **HURT SOMEONE** WITH ONE OF HIS DANGEROUSLY FAST PITCHES...

HE'S DOING IT AGAIN...

...A FACT COBB USED TO HIS ADVANTAGE BY **CROWDING THE PLATE** WHEN THE TWO FACED OFF. RATTLING JOHNSON, HE ADMITTED, WAS THE ONLY WAY HE COULD HIT HIM.

IS JOHNSON **CHIEFLY REMEMBERED** FOR HITTING MORE BATTERS THAN ANYBODY ELSE? OF COURSE NOT. HIS OTHER ASTOUNDING CAREER TOTALS (411 WINS, 2.17 LIFETIME E.R.A.) FAR OUTSHINE THIS RECORD, AND RIGHTLY SO. BUT IS IT POSSIBLE HE NEVER HAD THIS NOTORIETY BECAUSE -- IN SHARP CONTRAST WITH WHAT WAS ASSUMED ABOUT MAYS -- HE **HATED** HITTING GUYS... AND EVERYBODY KNEW IT?

AND THAT FATAL PITCH? EVEN TEAMMATES OF CHAPMAN'S HAD TO ADMIT IT WAS A STRIKE.

CHAPPIE TENDED TO HANG OVER THE PLATE..
SLIGHT SHIFTING OF LEFT FOOT
..AND APPEARED TO BE PREPARING TO BUNT.

MAYS FIRED IT IN ON THE HIGH SIDE...
..BUT CHAPMAN NEVER MOVED.

IT'S HARD TO BLAME A DEAD MAN, HARDER STILL ONE WHOM EVERYONE LIKED.

CARL MAYS WAS THE ONE LEFT STANDING IN THIS MATCH UP.

THE ONE WHO'D LIVE WITH THAT MOMENT'S EFFECTS FOR THE NEXT **FIFTY YEARS**.

IT WAS BAD LUCK ON BOTH SIDES...

...BUT RARELY HAS THERE BEEN A MORE **CONVENIENT** SCAPEGOAT.

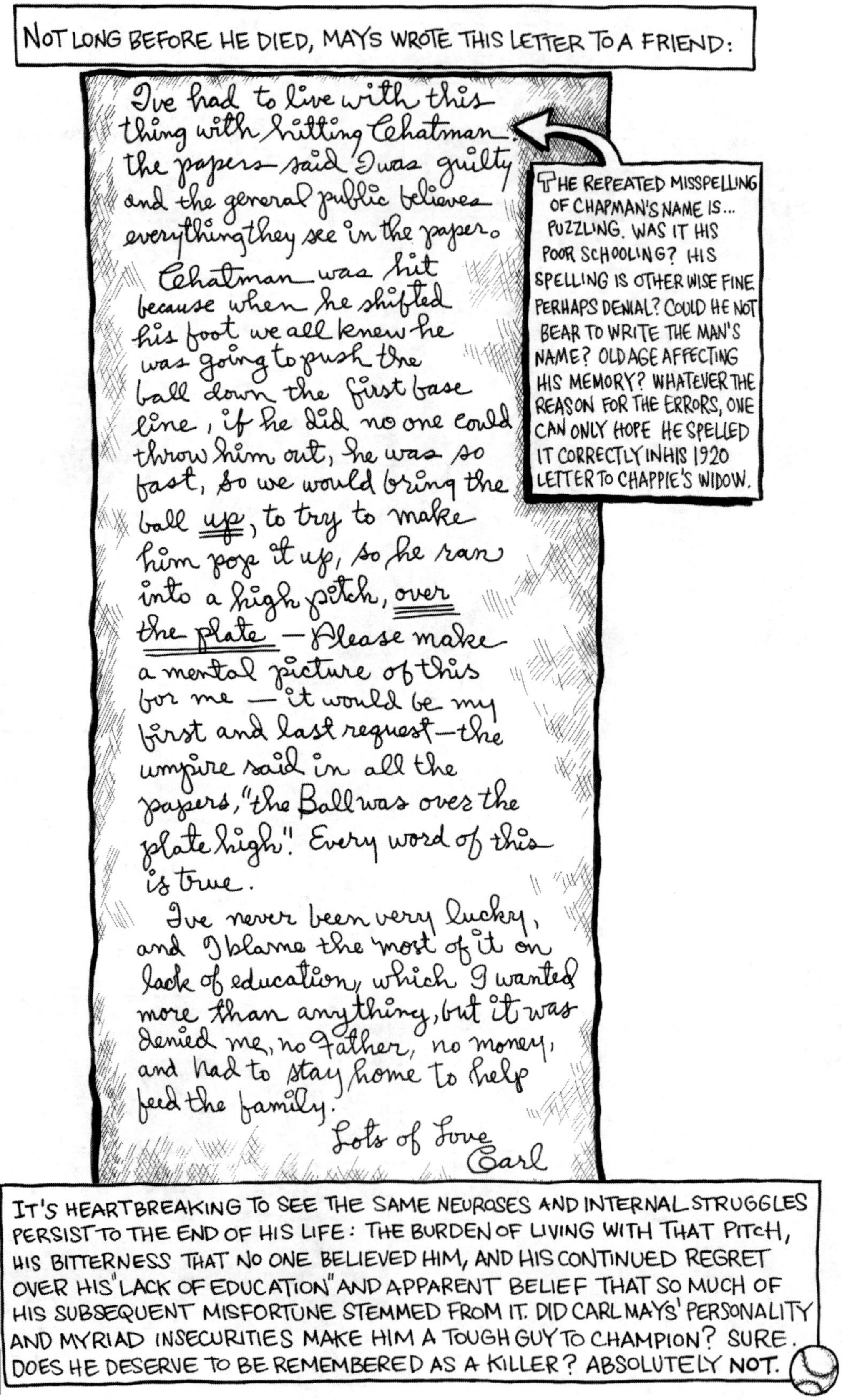

NOT LONG BEFORE HE DIED, MAYS WROTE THIS LETTER TO A FRIEND:

I've had to live with this thing with hitting Chatman. the papers said I was guilty and the general public believes everything they see in the paper.

Chatman was hit because when he shifted his foot we all knew he was going to push the ball down the first base line, if he did no one could throw him out, he was so fast, so we would bring the ball up, to try to make him pop it up, so he ran into a high pitch, over the plate — Please make a mental picture of this for me — it would be my first and last request — the umpire said in all the papers, "the Ball was over the plate high". Every word of this is true.

I've never been very lucky, and I blame the most of it on lack of education, which I wanted more than anything, but it was denied me, no Father, no money, and had to stay home to help feed the family.

Lots of Love
Carl

THE REPEATED MISSPELLING OF CHAPMAN'S NAME IS... PUZZLING. WAS IT HIS POOR SCHOOLING? HIS SPELLING IS OTHERWISE FINE. PERHAPS DENIAL? COULD HE NOT BEAR TO WRITE THE MAN'S NAME? OLD AGE AFFECTING HIS MEMORY? WHATEVER THE REASON FOR THE ERRORS, ONE CAN ONLY HOPE HE SPELLED IT CORRECTLY IN HIS 1920 LETTER TO CHAPPIE'S WIDOW.

IT'S HEARTBREAKING TO SEE THE SAME NEUROSES AND INTERNAL STRUGGLES PERSIST TO THE END OF HIS LIFE: THE BURDEN OF LIVING WITH THAT PITCH, HIS BITTERNESS THAT NO ONE BELIEVED HIM, AND HIS CONTINUED REGRET OVER HIS "LACK OF EDUCATION" AND APPARENT BELIEF THAT SO MUCH OF HIS SUBSEQUENT MISFORTUNE STEMMED FROM IT. DID CARL MAYS' PERSONALITY AND MYRIAD INSECURITIES MAKE HIM A TOUGH GUY TO CHAMPION? SURE. DOES HE DESERVE TO BE REMEMBERED AS A KILLER? ABSOLUTELY NOT.

"WAMBY" tells a tale.

17

IN WHICH CLEVELAND'S (ONLY) SEMINARIAN-TURNED-SECOND-BASEMAN REVEALS THE (MODERATELY) UNKNOWN RELIGOUS DISPUTE THAT (NEARLY) TORE THE TEAM ASUNDER.

HELLO THERE! I'M BILL WAMBSGANSS. BUT PLEASE: CALL ME **WAMBY**. YOU MIGHT AS WELL, EVERYONE ELSE DOES! AND YES, I AM INDEED THE **"UNASSISTED TRIPLE PLAY IN THE WORLD SERIES"** FELLOW.

YEP, MY OFT-ABBREVIATED NAME AND THAT PLAY: MY TWO CLAIMS TO FAME. IT COULD BE WORSE. I'M STILL PRETTY PROUD OF THAT PLAY. MY NAME--WELL, I CAN'T EXACTLY TAKE CREDIT FOR THAT.

AS YOU CAN SEE BY THAT BLACK ARMBAND, IT WAS 1920-- THE YEAR WE **LOST** RAY CHAPMAN AND **WON** THE CHAMPIONSHIP.

WE PLAYED IN THAT INFIELD TOGETHER FOR SIX YEARS. I STILL REMEMBER THIS LITTLE DITTY RING LARDNER, THE GREAT SPORTSWRITER, WROTE WHEN I JOINED THE CLUB. HE CAPTURED THE GIST OF MY SITUATION PRETTY WELL:

The team's nickname at the time

The Naps bought a shortstop named Wambsganss,
Who is slated to fill Ray Chapman's pants.
But when he saw Ray
And the way he could play
He muttered, "I haven't a clam's chance!"

GUESS I'D BETTER LEARN HOW TO PLAY SECOND...

POOR CHAPPIE! I'M SURE YOU'VE HEARD NO END OF PRAISE OF THE MAN—HOW HE WAS EVERYBODY'S BEST FRIEND—BUT IT WAS TRUE! HE REALLY KNEW HOW TO MAKE A GUY FEEL GOOD. YOU KNOW WHAT HE USED TO SAY ABOUT ME?

I'LL NEVER PLAY ALONGSIDE ANOTHER SECOND BASEMAN. WAMBY IS **IT**!
OH, BOY... THERE HE GOES AGAIN!
I MEAN IT! **NEVER**. I REFUSE!

AND YOU KNOW WHAT? **HE NEVER DID.**

AFTER HE DIED, WE WERE A MESS, AS YOU CAN PROBABLY IMAGINE. I'VE NEVER SEEN SO MANY GROWN MEN CRY.

... AND HOPE I NEVER DO AGAIN.

AND THEN THINGS GOT SO **UGLY** WITH --

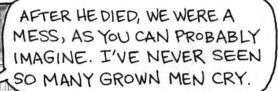

THOSE THREE-- TRIS SPEAKER, JACK GRANEY, AND STEVE O'NEILL-- WERE CHAPPIE'S CLOSEST BUDDIES ON THE TEAM, SO IT MADE SENSE THAT THEY WERE THE MOST AFFECTED WHEN THE UNTHINKABLE OCCURRED.

The Cleveland Indians were well-represented at the wedding of shortstop Ray Chapman to socialite Kathleen Daly. Above, from left to right: team player-manager-best man Tris Speaker; the newlyweds; catcher Steve O'Neill; leftfielder Jack Graney.

GRANEY AND O'NEILL COLLAPSED WHEN THEY SAW THE BODY AT THE VIEWING.

AND SPOKE? WELL, SO ACUTE WAS HIS PAIN AND EXHAUSTION IN THE WAKE OF HIS DEAR FRIEND'S DEATH THAT HE SUFFERED A **NERVOUS BREAKDOWN.**

HE'S HAD A TERRIBLE SHOCK...
CHAPPIE...
...IS THIS REALLY THE TRIS SPEAKER?

The mighty Grey Eagle, under a doctor's care at the home of Chapman's in-laws, the Dalys.

THE FUNERAL WAS ORIGINALLY TO TAKE PLACE AT THE CHAPEL WHERE RAY AND KATY HAD SO RECENTLY BEEN MARRIED, BUT WAS MOVED IN HOPES OF ACCOMMODATING THE LARGE NUMBERS EXPECTED TO ATTEND. THAT'S HOW IT CAME TO BE HELD AT ST. JOHN'S--A ROMAN CATHOLIC CHURCH.

LET'S JUST SAY THAT THIS DIDN'T SIT VERY WELL WITH SPOKE. MUCH HAS BEEN SAID OF... HMM... HOW SHALL I PUT THIS.. HE WAS **ZEALOUSLY PROTESTANT** BACK THEN. BETWEEN THE LOCALE OF THE SERVICE AND THE NEWS FROM KATHLEEN THAT RAY **CONVERTED TO CATHOLICISM** ON HIS DEATHBED...

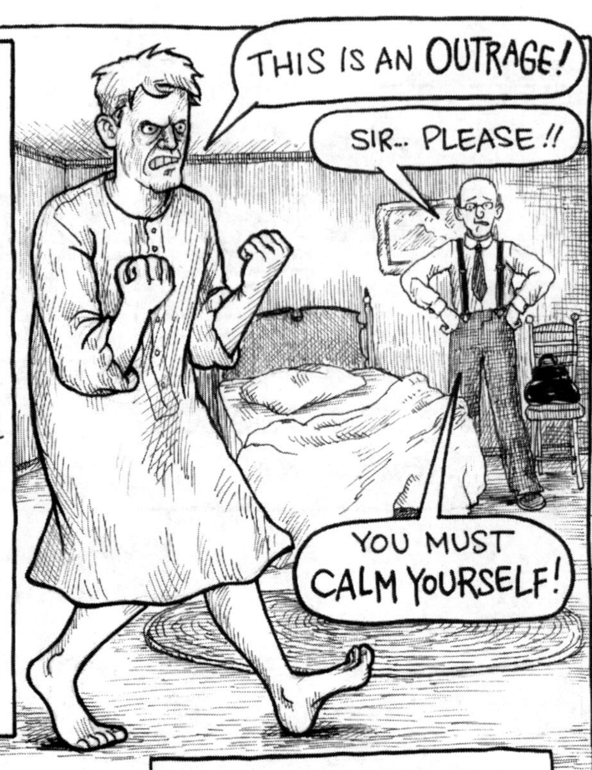
THIS IS AN OUTRAGE!
SIR.. PLEASE!!
YOU MUST CALM YOURSELF!

.. IT WAS A BIT TOO MUCH FOR HIM.

GRANEY AND O'NEILL, ON THE OTHER HAND, WERE **CATHOLIC**.

First Holy Communion.
Little Steve O'Neill
Little Jack Graney

THERE HAD BEEN TENSION BETWEEN CATHOLICS AND PROTESTANTS IN OUR CLUBHOUSE BEFORE (THERE OFTEN WAS WHEN SPEAKER WAS INVOLVED) BUT CHAPPIE, RAISED PROTESTANT BUT MARRIED TO A CATHOLIC WOMAN, HAD BEEN A **UNIFYING ELEMENT**.

CHAPPIE COULD NO LONGER PLAY PEACEMAKER, AND SO THINGS QUICKLY DETERIORATED. OF THE THREE OF THOSE TEAMMATES THAT ATTENDED HIS WEDDING, JUST ONE, STEVE O'NEILL, WAS PRESENT AT HIS FUNERAL.

WHEW! NO ONE'S NOTICED.
STEVE'S GOT A **SHINER**!
(YES, EXPLANATION OF BLACK EYE FORTHCOMING...)

WHERE WERE GRANEY AND SPOKE? THE STORY WAS THAT THEY WERE UNABLE TO FACE THE FINAL GOODBYE: SPOKE STILL IN BED, ON THE VERGE OF MADNESS WITH GRIEF; GRANEY TAKEN OUT OF TOWN TO RECUPERATE BY NO LESS ESCORT THAN NAP LAJOIE. THEY WERE "TOO OVERCOME" TO ATTEND.

LET'S GO FOR A RIDE, JACK.
NAPOLEON LAJOIE, CLEVELAND'S LEGENDARY SECOND BASEMAN (1902-1914) AND MANAGER (1905-1909)

WHILE THEY CERTAINLY WERE OVERCOME, THERE WERE OTHER FORCES AT WORK. THE REAL REASON THAT SPOKE AND GRANEY MISSED THEIR BEST FRIEND'S FUNERAL? IT SEEMED THAT IT WAS IN NO SMALL PART DUE TO THE FACT THAT THEY HAD ATTEMPTED TO BEAT THE BEJESUS OUT OF EACH OTHER, AND PROBABLY COULDN'T STAND TO BE IN THE SAME ROOM.

OR AT THE VERY LEAST, SPOKE GAVE O'NEILL A LICKING. ONE WITNESS TO THE FIGHT RECALLED THE EXTENSIVE "FACIAL PUNISHMENT" O'NEILL RECEIVED COURTESY MR. SPEAKER. BUT WORD WAS THAT ALL THREE MEN WERE INVOLVED.

O'NEILL MISSED A COUPLE OF GAMES DUE TO A "BRUISED RIGHT HAND." (GUESS HE CONNECTED A FEW TIMES AFTER ALL...)

I'M NOT SAYING THEY WEREN'T DISTRAUGHT. SPEAKER CERTAINLY MAY HAVE HAD A NERVOUS BREAKDOWN. HE SURE LOOKED LIKE HE HAD WHEN HE REJOINED THE TEAM...
AND I'M PRETTY SURE THAT NAP LAJOIE WOULDN'T LIE ABOUT WHISKING GRANEY AWAY TO SEDATE HIM.

ALL RIGHT, BOYS...
LET'S PLAY SOME BALL.
(SIGH.)

BUT YOU WANT TO KNOW SOMETHING STRANGE? WHEN SPOKE FINALLY DID COME BACK, IN HIS VERY FIRST GAME AFTER THE FUNERAL, HE IMMEDIATELY TOOK BOTH O'NEILL AND GRANEY OUT OF THE LINEUP.
HE'S GOT SOME NERVE.
SHH!
COINCIDENCE? MAYBE. MAYBE NOT.

I ASKED GRANEY ABOUT THE WHOLE AFFAIR POINT BLANK ONE TIME. HE LOOKED AT ME AND KINDA LAUGHED:

HEH. NO, BILL...
THAT NEVER HAPPENED.

BUT I KNOW DAMN WELL IT DID.

THIS WHOLE AFFAIR IS RIDICULOUS AND PETTY, ESPECIALLY IN HINDSIGHT. BUT THINK ABOUT IT: PREJUDICES ASIDE, THEY WERE SHOCKED AND BEREAVED, AT ODDS OVER HOW BEST TO HONOR A DEAR FRIEND'S MEMORY.

COULD THEY HAVE BEEN FIGHTING OVER HIS FRIENDSHIP, EVEN AFTER HIS DEATH?

I GUESS WE'LL NEVER KNOW FOR SURE. FROM MY PERSPECTIVE, IT SEEMED THAT THOSE THREE WERE DESPERATE FOR ONE LAST CHANCE TO DO RIGHT BY CHAPPIE. KIND OF TOUCHING, WHEN YOU THINK ABOUT IT.

18

Filling Chappie's Shoes

IN ADDITION TO BEING COMPLETELY DEMORALIZED AFTER CHAPMAN'S DEATH, THE CLEVELAND TEAM WAS FACED WITH ANOTHER VERY PRESSING ISSUE:

THEY NEEDED A SHORTSTOP.

THEY WERE, AFTER ALL, STILL IN THE MIDST OF A PENNANT RACE AND SUDDENLY WITHOUT ONE OF THEIR **STARS**. THE VOID CHAPPIE LEFT OFF THE FIELD WAS, OF COURSE, **IMMEASURABLE**... BUT THE VOID HE LEFT ON THE FIELD WAS PRETTY BIG, TOO.

ENTER HARRY LUNTE, LITTLE-USED UTILITY INFIELDER!

WHY "LITTLE-USED"?

WELL, ASIDE FROM THE FACT THAT UP UNTIL THIS POINT THE INDIANS INFIELD HAD BEEN CHOCK-A-BLOCK WITH TALENTED PLAYERS...

... THERE WAS ALSO THE ISSUE THAT HARRY LUNTE'S HITTING LEFT SOMETHING TO BE DESIRED.

A <u>LOT</u> TO BE DESIRED, ACTUALLY.

NO, HARRY LUNTE COULDN'T **HIT** WORTH A DAMN... BUT BOY, COULD HE **FIELD**!

LUNTE'S REPUTATION AS YOUR BASIC "GOOD-FIELD-NO-HIT" PLAYER WAS CEMENTED EARLY. AFTER HIS FIRST APPEARANCE FOR THE INDIANS, THE PAPER LISTED HIS NAME THUSLY:

Bunte ss 2 0 0 2

EVEN AS HE BECAME A JOKE AT THE PLATE, HIS SKILL IN THE INFIELD GAINED HIM AT LEAST ONE ARDENT (AND **IMPORTANT**) ADMIRER....

BUT AS A STARTER? **NOW?** WHEN HE LOST CHAPPIE, SPEAKER FOUND THAT HE HAD NO OTHER OPTION.

SO... IT LOOKS LIKE IT'S GONNA HAVE TO BE BUN-- ER, SORRY-- LUNTE.
SIGH. WELL, THERE GOES THE PENNANT...
TEAM OWNER JIM DUNN

THE STILL-MOURNING FANS WERE SUPPORTIVE WHEN LUNTE FIRST STEPPED IN... BUT THEY REALLY WEREN'T EXPECTING MUCH.

MUCH TO, WELL, EVERYONE'S SURPRISE, LUNTE TURNED OUT TO BE A NEARLY ADEQUATE REPLACEMENT...

NICE WORK, LUNTE!

... FOR TWO WHOLE WEEKS.

SO UNUSED TO RUNNING BASES WAS POOR LUNTE THAT, WHILE ROUNDING FIRST AFTER A RARE BASE HIT, HE PULLED A MUSCLE IN HIS LEG AND HAD TO BE HELPED OFF THE FIELD.

OW!

AND THUS ENDED HIS SHOT AT CHAPMAN'S SADLY VACATED POST -- AND SO THE SEARCH WENT ON.

THESE WERE **DESPERATE** TIMES.

THERE WERE RUMORS ABOUT A KID IN THE FARM SYSTEM NAMED JOE SEWELL: TWENTY-ONE, 5'6", AND WITH A GRAND TOTAL OF **FOUR MONTHS** UNDER HIS BELT IN THE MINOR LEAGUES.

SPEAKER WAS UTTERLY UNCONVINCED THAT THIS SEWELL FELLOW WAS READY FOR THE MAJOR LEAGUES — AND A **PENNANT RACE**, NO LESS! — BUT WHAT ELSE COULD HE DO?

MEANWHILE, IN NEW ORLEANS, THE INDIANS' PROSPECT WAS JUST AS ENTHUSIASTIC AS HIS SOON-TO-BE MANAGER ABOUT HIS PROMOTION...

... THAT IS, NOT VERY.

UNCONVINCED (BUT UNABLE TO REFUSE), THE RELUCTANT REPLACEMENT WAS OFF TO CLEVELAND.

DURING A LAYOVER ON HIS JOURNEY, HE FINALLY FOUND A WAY TO PUT HIS INSECURITIES TO REST.

IT WORKED. JOE SEWELL NOT ONLY FILLED CHAPPIE'S SHOES, BUT BECAME A **STAR**. HE WENT ON TO PLAY FOR THIRTEEN DISTINGUISHED YEARS IN THE MAJOR LEAGUES.

AND IN THE END, HIS CAREER ECLIPSED THAT OF THE MAN HE'D BEEN CALLED ON TO REPLACE.

19

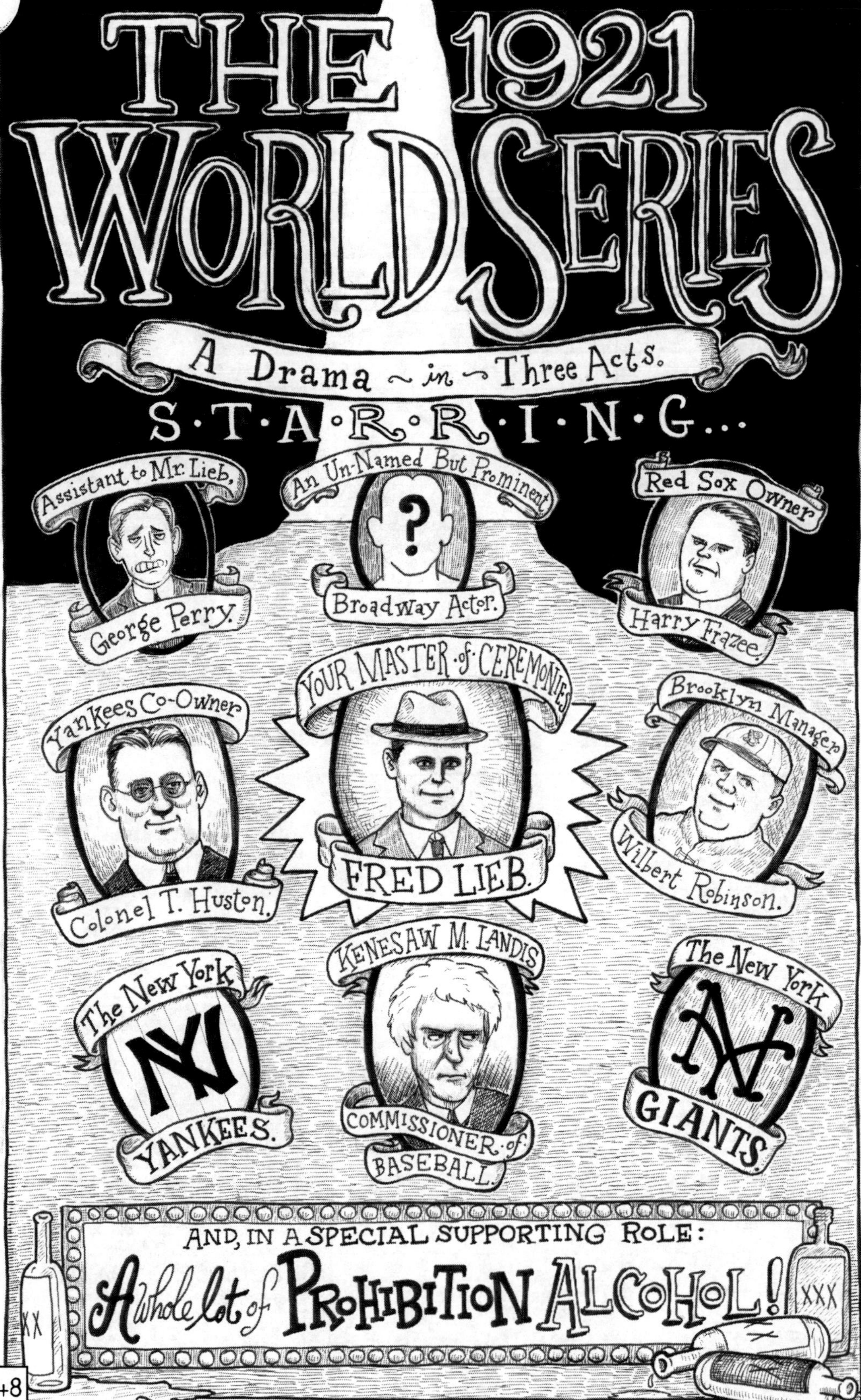
THE 1921 WORLD SERIES
A Drama ~ in ~ Three Acts.
S·T·A·R·R·I·N·G...
Assistant to Mr. Lieb,
George Perry.
An Un-Named But Prominent
Broadway Actor.
Red Sox Owner
Harry Frazee.
YOUR MASTER of CEREMONIES
FRED LIEB.
Yankees Co-Owner
Colonel T. Huston.
Brooklyn Manager
Wilbert Robinson.
The New York
YANKEES.
KENESAW M. LANDIS
COMMISSIONER of BASEBALL.
The New York
GIANTS.
AND, IN A SPECIAL SUPPORTING ROLE:
A whole lot of PROHIBITION ALCOHOL!

GREETINGS, FUTURE BASEBALL ENTHUSIASTS! I'M FRED LIEB.* BE WARNED: THE STORY I'M ABOUT TO TELL MAY SHOCK YOU. CARL MAYS, LONG ASSUMED TO HAVE BEEN EXCLUDED FROM BASEBALL'S HALL OF FAME FOR REASONS RELATED TO HIS FATAL BEANING OF RAY CHAPMAN....
*LEGENDARY BASEBALL WRITER

...MAY HE REST IN PEACE...

... HAS NOT, I CAN NOW REVEAL, BEEN KEPT FROM THE HALL DUE TO HIS CONNECTION TO THIS UNHAPPY EVENT...
..BUT ON OTHER GROUNDS ENTIRELY...

WHICH I WILL DETAIL FOR YOU NOW.

ACT ONE: New York City, 1921.

THE 1921 WORLD SERIES: THE VERY **FIRST TIME** TWO NEW YORK TEAMS FACED EACH OTHER IN BASEBALL'S CHAMPIONSHIP SERIES!

TO SAY THE CITY WAS CAUGHT UP IN THE EXCITEMENT WOULD BE QUITE THE UNDERSTATEMENT— AND AS A NEW YORK SPORTSWRITER, I FOUND MYSELF WITH AN EMBARRASSMENT OF RICHES.

1921: His Best-Ever Season
MAYS: UNAFFECTED BY LAST SUMMER'S TRAGEDY?

THE YANKEES' CARL MAYS WAS COMING OFF A DOMINANT YEAR. HE'D WON **27 GAMES** – TIED FOR THE MOST IN ALL OF BASEBALL – AND HAD DEALT THE GIANTS A 5-HIT SHUTOUT IN GAME ONE OF THE SERIES, LEADING HIS TEAM TO A 3-0 WIN. THE YANKS AND GIANTS SPLIT THE NEXT TWO DECISIONS, AND MAYS WAS CALLED ON AGAIN TO PITCH GAME FOUR.

MAYS STARTED OUT MASTERFULLY, HOLDING MCGRAW'S LADS TO TWO-HIT BALL FOR SEVEN INNINGS.

UGH!

MEANWHILE THE YANKEES HAD MANAGED A RUN, AND THE SCORE STOOD AT 1–0. THE TROUBLE BEGAN IN THE EIGHTH.
NICKNAME: "IRISH"
EMIL MEUSEL WAS UP.

YANKEES MANAGER MILLER HUGGINS SIGNALED THE PITCH HE WANTED MAYS TO DELIVER FROM THE DUGOUT.
FASTBALL, APPARENTLY.

WHATEVER, HUG.
MAYS IGNORED HUGGINS, AND THREW A SLOW-BREAKING CURVE...
... WHICH IRISH ANSWERED WITH A TRIPLE, AND SOON SCORED.

THE INNING RESULTED IN A RUN-SCORING SINGLE, A SACRIFICE BUNT (MISHANDLED BY MAYS), AND A DOUBLE.
THE GIANTS HAD TAKEN A 3-1 LEAD.

THEY SCORED ANOTHER RUN IN THE NINTH OFF A COUPLE MORE HITS. BABE RUTH HIT A HOME RUN IN THE BOTTOM OF THE NINTH...
... BUT THAT WAS ALL THE YANKEES COULD MUSTER...

GIANTS
... AND THE GAME WENT TO THE GIANTS, 4-2.

HUGGINS WAS ABSOLUTELY **FURIOUS** WITH MAYS FOR GOING ROGUE ON HIM WHEN HE THREW THE BREAKING BALL TO IRISH MEUSEL. THAT TRIPLE TURNED THE GAME AROUND, AND HE WAS **CERTAIN** THAT IT COULD HAVE BEEN PREVENTED.

BUT THE GAME WAS OVER, AND IT WAS NOW TIME TO LOOK AHEAD TO GAME FIVE....

... OR SO I THOUGHT.

THAT NIGHT AROUND MIDNIGHT, MY COLLEAGUE **GEORGE PERRY**, WHO WAS ASSISTING ME WITH HOSPITALITY FOR THE NATIONAL PRESS, APPROACHED ME AT THE HOTEL.

HE WAS ACCOMPANIED BY A PROMINENT BROADWAY ACTOR, WHOSE IDENTITY I **WILL NOT REVEAL**.

OK, LET'S JUST SAY HE LOOKED LIKE **THIS**:

FRED, YOU'VE **GOT** TO HEAR THIS MAN'S STORY.

THE ACTOR PROCEEDED TO TELL **QUITE** A TALE.

ACCORDING TO THE ACTOR, SOME PEOPLE WHO "REGARDED A GIANTS VICTORY AS ABSOLUTELY NECESSARY TO THEIR WELFARE" **PROMISED CARL MAYS A SUM OF MONEY** IF HE'D OFFER ENOUGH HITTABLE PITCHES TO **LOSE A CLOSE GAME**...

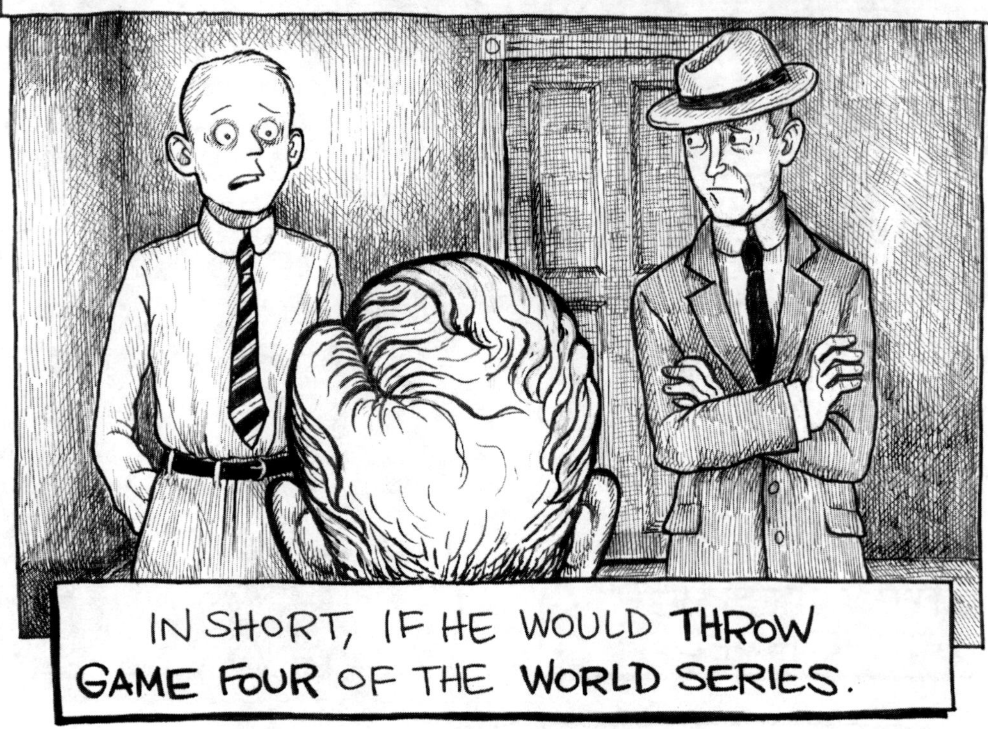

IN SHORT, IF HE WOULD THROW GAME FOUR OF THE WORLD SERIES.

THE ACTOR WENT ON TO EXPLAIN THAT **MAYS' WIFE**, WHO WAS SEATED IN THE GRANDSTAND THAT DAY, WAS TO **LIFT A WHITE HANDKERCHIEF** TO HER FACE TO SIGNAL TO HER HUSBAND THAT THE MONEY HAD BEEN HANDED OVER AND HE WAS TO COMMENCE HIS PART IN THE PLOY.

HE CLAIMED THAT MRS. MAYS HAD **GIVEN THE SIGNAL** AT THE TOP OF THE EIGHTH INNING — AFTER WHICH HER HUSBAND HAD PROCEEDED TO **IGNORE** HUGGINS' SIGNAL, AND GIVE UP THREE RUNS.

WHY WOULD HE TAKE THE CHANCE?

HE'D HAVE TO BE **CRAZY**!

BASEBALL WAS STILL REELING FROM THE "BLACK SOX" RULING A YEAR BEFORE.

the **1919** *White Sox*

THE COMMISSIONER OF BASEBALL HAD ADOPTED A **ZERO-TOLERANCE** STANCE ON CHEATING AND GAMBLING.

AS UNLIKELY AS IT SEEMED, I KNEW I HAD TO TAKE THE STORY SERIOUSLY. SO PERRY, THE ACTOR, AND I HEADED OVER TO THE YANKEES' CO-OWNER COLONEL HUSTON'S HOTEL NEARBY.

WE FOUND HUSTON, ALONG WITH HIS FRIEND HARRY FRAZEE, IN HIS SUITE. THEY WERE ASLEEP, AND **DRUNK**.

ONCE I MANAGED TO AWAKEN THE COLONEL (NO SMALL FEAT, AS IT TURNED OUT), I GOT THE ACTOR TO **REPEAT THE STORY**.

RIGHT. OKAY... THIS DOESN'T LOOK TOO GOOD FOR OUR CLUB.
HAVE YOU TOLD **LANDIS***?
Z-Z-Z-Z-Z-

* KENESAW MOUNTAIN LANDIS, COMMISSIONER OF BASEBALL

I TOLD HIM THAT WAS OUR NEXT STOP, AND SO HE JOINED US.

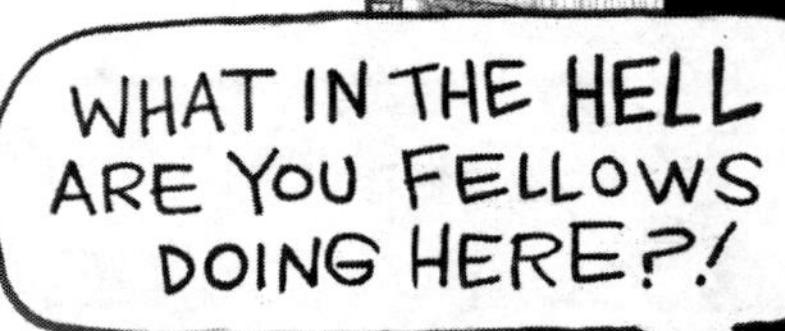

WHAT IN THE **HELL** ARE YOU FELLOWS DOING HERE?!

I WOULDN'T SAY THAT LANDIS WAS **THRILLED** TO SEE US...

JUDGE, THIS MAN THINKS MAYS **LET UP** IN THE LAST TWO INNINGS.

COME IN.

LANDIS GRILLED THE ACTOR **EXHAUSTIVELY** ON THE DETAILS OF HIS STORY...
NOW, THIS **HANDKERCHIEF**...
YOU SAY IT WAS **WHITE**?

...AND **APPARENTLY** THOUGHT THERE MIGHT BE SOMETHING TO IT, AS HE PULLED ME ASIDE BEFORE WE FINALLY LEFT.
I'M **HIRING A DETECTIVE**, FRED.
DON'T REPORT THIS UNTIL THERE ARE FURTHER DEVELOPMENTS.

THE NEXT TIME MAYS PITCHED, THE GIANTS WON AGAIN, 2-1, ON A SEVENTH-INNING DOUBLE.

NEW YORK

I DIDN'T HEAR FROM LANDIS AGAIN UNTIL THE SERIES – WHICH THE GIANTS WON – WAS OVER.

THE DETECTIVE DIDN'T FIND ANYTHING, FRED.

HE'S **CLEAN.**
HM. ALL RIGHT, THEN.

AND SO I **FILED IT AWAY** WITH ALL THOSE OTHER RUMORS THAT FLOAT AROUND BASEBALL AT ANY GIVEN TIME, AND FORGOT ABOUT IT ENTIRELY, **UNTIL**...

Act Two: Georgia, 1928

MY WIFE AND I WERE PART OF A GROUP VISITING A HUNTING LODGE IN BRUNSWICK, GEORGIA. SEVERAL BASEBALL TEAM OWNERS CO-OWNED THE PLACE.

IT WAS THE OFF-SEASON, AND THE MAIN ACTIVITY FOR MOST OF THE GUESTS THAT PARTICULAR WEEKEND WAS PUTTING AWAY "RUM AND COCA-COLAS" BY THE FIRE.

GLUG
I MAY OR MAY NOT HAVE PARTAKEN.

AMONG THOSE IN ATTENDANCE WERE COLONEL HUSTON AND BROOKLYN MANAGER WILBERT ROBINSON (OR "UNCLE ROBBIE", AS EVERYONE CALLED HIM)

WELL, IF IT ISN'T MISTER LIEB!
FREDDY!
WE'RE "OFF THE RECORD," RIGHT?

THE RUM HAD PUT THE COLONEL IN A **CONFESSIONAL** STATE OF MIND, AND AFTER WE HAD BEEN SITTING AND CHATTING FOR A WHILE, HE LEANED IN TOWARDS ME AND SAID:

FRED...
I AM ABOUT TO TELL YOU THE DAMNEDEST STORY A BASEBALL OWNER EVER TOLD A REPORTER.

OH?
WELL, THAT SURE GOT MY ATTENTION.
YOU DON'T SAY.

AND IT GOT UNCLE ROBBIE'S, TOO. HE HAD NEARLY SLIPPED INTO A **DRUNKEN REVERIE**, BUT THIS SNAPPED HIM OUT OF IT IMMEDIATELY.

SHHHH!!
NO, COLONEL! DON'T TELL HIM! DON'T TELL HIM!

FOR A WHILE THIS PATTERN REPEATED. THE COLONEL WOULD DANGLE THE STORY BEFORE ME, UNCLE ROBBIE WOULD BECOME APOPLECTIC, THE SUBJECT WOULD BE **DROPPED**.

THE REVELLERS BEGAN TO DROP OFF ONE BY ONE, AND EVENTUALLY — **MERCIFULLY** — UNCLE ROBBIE WAS **SILENCED**...
Z-Z-Z-Z-Z Z-Z-Z-Z
... SO TO SPEAK.
OFF TO BED, ROBBIE!

IT WOULDN'T BE LONG NOW! UNFORTUNATELY, THERE WAS **ANOTHER SPORTSWRITER** WITHIN EARSHOT WHO HAD OVERHEARD THE THREE OF US. HE WANTED IN ON THIS **JUICY TALE** -- WHATEVER IT WAS -- AS WELL.
OH, I'M **ON TO YOU**, BUDDY...
I COULDN'T REALLY **BLAME** HIM. BUT I WANTED THE SCOOP, AND THE COLONEL WOULDN'T TELL ME WHILE THIS **NOSY FELLOW** WAS HANGING AROUND.

AND THEN THE RUM CLAIMED HIM, TOO.

I TURNED TO THE COLONEL. "NOW THAT WE'RE ALONE," I SAID, "**WHAT** IS THIS STORY YOU'RE HOLDING OUT ON ME?"

UNFORTUNATELY, BY THIS TIME HE WAS MOMENTS AWAY FROM JOINING UNCLE ROBBIE AND THE OTHERS IN AN INTOXICATED DREAMLAND.

I WANTED TO TELL YOU...

...THAT SOME OF OUR PITCHERS THREW GAMES ON US IN BOTH 1921 AND 1922.
(HIC!)

YOU MEAN THE MAYS MATTER OF THE 1921 WORLD SERIES?

BUT BY THEN HE WAS DONE SHARING...

...AND STAGGERED OFF TO BED.

WE HAD TO LEAVE VERY EARLY THE NEXT MORNING. UNSURPRISINGLY, THE COLONEL WAS STILL SLEEPING IT OFF, SO THERE WAS **NO CHANCE** FOR ANY FOLLOW-UP QUESTIONING.

THE NEXT TIME I SPOKE TO HIM ALONE—NEARLY A YEAR LATER—ALL I COULD GET OUT OF HIM WAS, **"I STAND BY WHAT I TOLD YOU THAT NIGHT."**

THAT CARL MAYS HAD, INDEED, DONE HIS PART TO THROW THE 1921 WORLD SERIES.

ACT THREE: New York City, 1929.

WHILE CHATTING WITH MILLER HUGGINS AND A COUPLE OF OTHER WRITERS, TALK TURNED TO THE **SAD SITUATION** IN WHICH MANY EX-BALLPLAYERS FOUND THEMSELVES FINANCIALLY. BACK THEN, THERE WAS NO SUCH THING AS A RETIREMENT CHECK FOR THESE FELLOWS, AND A NUMBER FOUND THEMSELVES IN **DIRE STRAITS** ONCE THEIR PLAYING CAREERS WERE OVER.

HUGGINS, MOVED, PLEDGED THAT HIS MEN WOULD ALWAYS HAVE SOMEWHERE TO TURN.

ANY BALLPLAYERS WHO PLAYED FOR ME COULD COME TO ME IF THEY WERE IN NEED.
I'D GIVE THEM A HELPING HAND.

THEN HE **PAUSED.**

I MAKE ONLY TWO EXCEPTIONS:

CARL MAYS AND JOE BUSH.

IF THEY WERE IN THE GUTTER...

I'D KICK THEM!

AND THERE WAS NO DOUBT IN OUR MINDS THAT HE WOULD, TOO.

I WAS REASONABLY SURE WHAT LED TO HIS HATRED OF PITCHER "BULLET JOE" BUSH...

1922 WORLD SERIES.
(HUG SIGNALS TO WALK THE BATTER)
?
(BUSH)
WHAT FOR,
YOU STUPID $#%?!
I WAS THERE. I'M FAIRLY SURE EVERYONE AT THE BALLPARK HEARD HIM.
DADDY?
WHAT DOES "$#%?" MEAN?

BUT WHAT ABOUT **MAYS**? WHAT COULD HE HAVE DONE THAT WOULD HAVE **ENRAGED** HUG AS MUCH AS THIS DISRESPECTFUL STUNT DID? PERHAPS... **THROW THE '21 WORLD SERIES**?

MAYS REMAINED WITH THE YANKEES FOR TWO MORE SEASONS AFTER 1921'S **DEBACLE**, AND HIS AND HUG'S RELATIONSHIP DETERIORATED STEADILY DURING THAT TIME. AFTER THAT STELLAR 27-9 SEASON IN 1921, HE MANAGED ONLY A BLEAK 13 WINS, 14 LOSSES DURING THE '22 SEASON.

IN 1923, HUGGINS **BARELY** USED HIM.

THE CLUB WAIVED MAYS AFTER THE 1923 WORLD SERIES (WHICH, INCIDENTALLY, THE YANKEES WON WITHOUT USING HIM AT ALL) AND THE CINCINNATI REDS PICKED HIM UP.

HUGGINS THEN WROTE TO REDS PRESIDENT (AND OLD FRIEND) GARRY HERMANN.

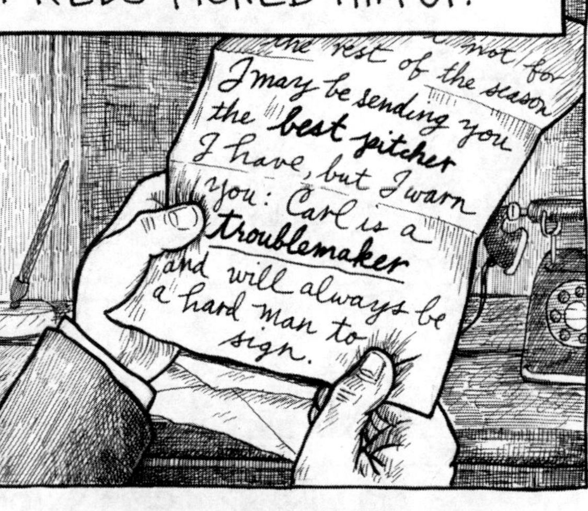

the rest of the season
I may be sending you
the best pitcher
I have, but I warn
you: Carl is a
troublemaker
and will always be
a hard man to
sign.

THAT'S RIGHT-- HIS **BEST** PITCHER. KEEP IN MIND THAT THE YANKEES' PITCHING ROSTER AT THAT TIME INCLUDED **TWO** FUTURE HALL-OF-FAMERS.

And finally...
Epilogue.

LOOKING BACK, I'M SOMEHOW STILL RELUCTANT TO CONDEMN MAYS, DESPITE EVERYTHING I'VE SEEN AND HEARD!

$#?@!
AFTER ALL, IN 1921 COMMISSIONER LANDIS DECLARED HIM CLEAN--
(KENESAW MOUNTAIN LANDIS: TOUGH ON DIRTY PLAYERS... AND GOLF BALLS)

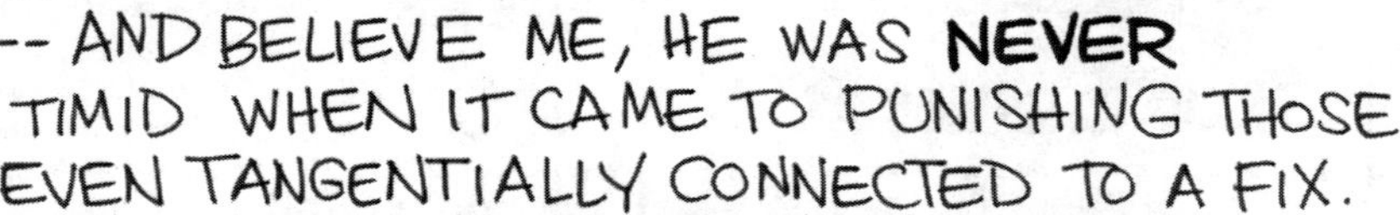
-- AND BELIEVE ME, HE WAS NEVER TIMID WHEN IT CAME TO PUNISHING THOSE EVEN TANGENTIALLY CONNECTED TO A FIX.

AND YET, SO MANY QUESTIONS AND SUSPICIONS REMAIN. BUT NOW I'VE TOLD YOU ALL I KNOW...
... AND YOU CAN JUDGE CARL MAYS FOR YOURSELVES.

20

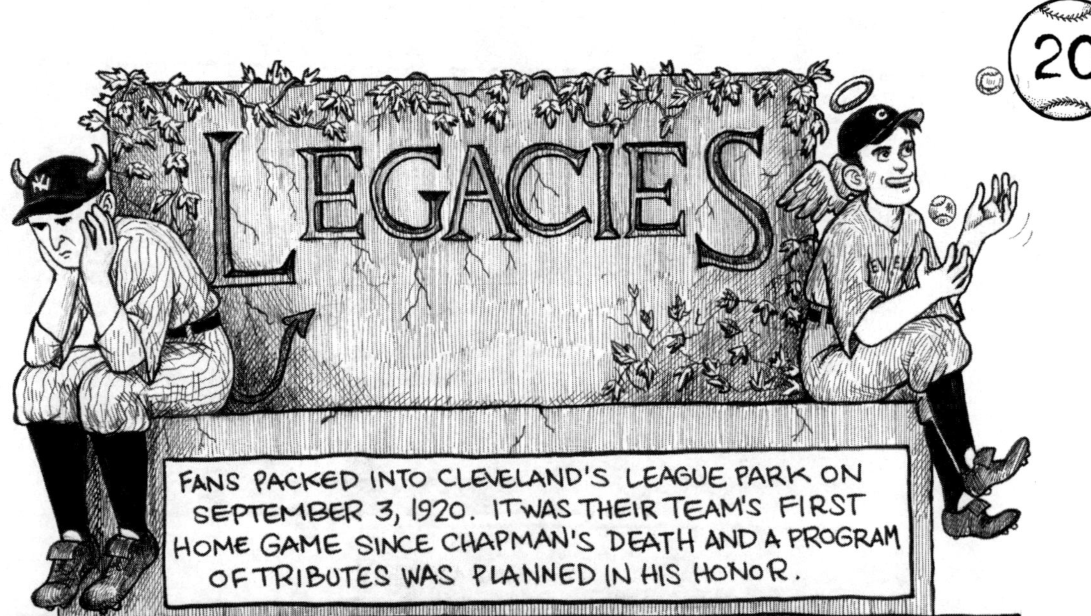

LEGACIES
FANS PACKED INTO CLEVELAND'S LEAGUE PARK ON SEPTEMBER 3, 1920. IT WAS THEIR TEAM'S FIRST HOME GAME SINCE CHAPMAN'S DEATH AND A PROGRAM OF TRIBUTES WAS PLANNED IN HIS HONOR.

BEFORE THE START OF THE GAME, A SAILOR FROM CHAPPIE'S OLD UNIT SLOWLY WALKED OUT TO THE SHORTSTOP POSITION PLAYING "TAPS."

THERE WASN'T A DRY EYE IN THE BALLPARK.

KATHLEEN CHAPMAN DIDN'T ATTEND, AND WOULDN'T ATTEND ANOTHER BALLGAME FOR AS LONG AS SHE LIVED. SHE WROTE A STATEMENT THAT APPEARED IN THE MEMORIAL PAMPHLET DISTRIBUTED THAT DAY...

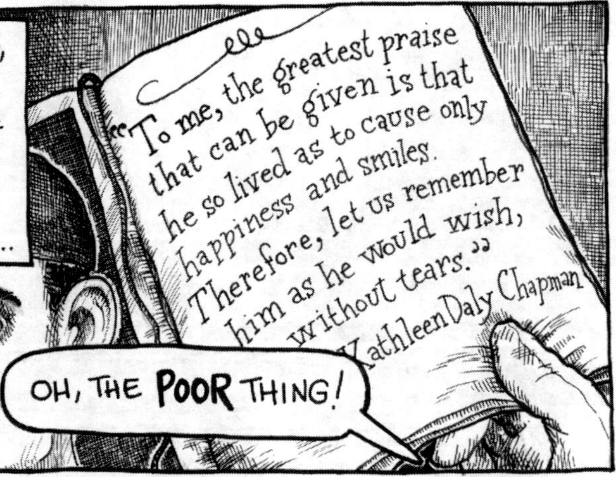

"To me, the greatest praise that can be given is that he so lived as to cause only happiness and smiles. Therefore, let us remember him as he would wish, without tears."
Kathleen Daly Chapman
OH, THE **POOR** THING!

AS STRONG AND SUNNY AS SHE APPEARED IN PRINT, KATY WAS INCONSOLABLE. CONCERN FOR HER UNBORN CHILD'S WELFARE PULLED HER THROUGH...

SHE LOOKS JUST LIKE HIM!

...AND ON FEBRUARY 27, 1921, RAE MARIE CHAPMAN WAS BORN. WHEN LITTLE RAE WAS TWO, KATY MARRIED AGAIN—TO A COUSIN, JOSEPH—AND THE THREE OF THEM MOVED TO CALIFORNIA.

BUT WHAT HAD SEEMED LIKE A FRESH START BECAME JUST ANOTHER SAD-FATED CHAPTER IN THE CHAPMAN STORY WHEN, IN 1928, SHE COMMITTED SUICIDE. SHE HAD INGESTED POISON.

RAE WAS SENT BACK TO CLEVELAND TO LIVE WITH HER GRANDPARENTS. ALMOST EXACTLY A YEAR LATER, SHE CONTRACTED THE MEASLES AND DIED. SHE WAS EIGHT YEARS OLD.

CLEVELAND DAILY NEWS

"The boys had a tough time of it getting squared away following Chapman's death. It was the hardest battle I've ever had in my life to overcome my grief... But we realized that all our tears and heartache couldn't bring dear Ray back, and we just pulled ourselves together with that which was ever uppermost in Chappie's mind — the pennant and world's championship — as our goal." — T. Speaker, Mgr / Cntrfldr

AFTER CHAPPIE'S DEATH, THE INDIANS STILL HAD A SEASON TO FINISH — AND TRIS SPEAKER WAS DETERMINED TO MAKE IT WORTHY OF HIS FRIEND'S MEMORY.

AND THAT HE DID. IT WAS A TALL ORDER IN GENERAL — THE SHAKEN CLEVELAND SQUAD HAD LOST A KEY PLAYER, THE VERY GLUE THAT HELD THEIR CLUBHOUSE TOGETHER. THE COMPETITION WAS STIFF, BUT THEY PLAYED HARD, FIRST FENDING OFF CHALLENGES FROM THE YANKEES AND SCANDAL-RIDDEN WHITE SOX IN THE AMERICAN LEAGUE...

FIRST PENNANT IN INDIANS HISTORY! HOW DO YOU FEEL, SPOKE?
TIRED. SO TIRED.

...THEN DEFEATING THE BROOKLYN DODGERS IN THE WORLD SERIES.

Manager Speaker embraces his mother moments after the Indians win their first World Series, October 12, 1920.

THE GRIEVING CITY TOOK SOME COMFORT IN THE FACT THAT CHAPPIE WAS SURELY LOOKING DOWN ON THEM WITH PRIDE.

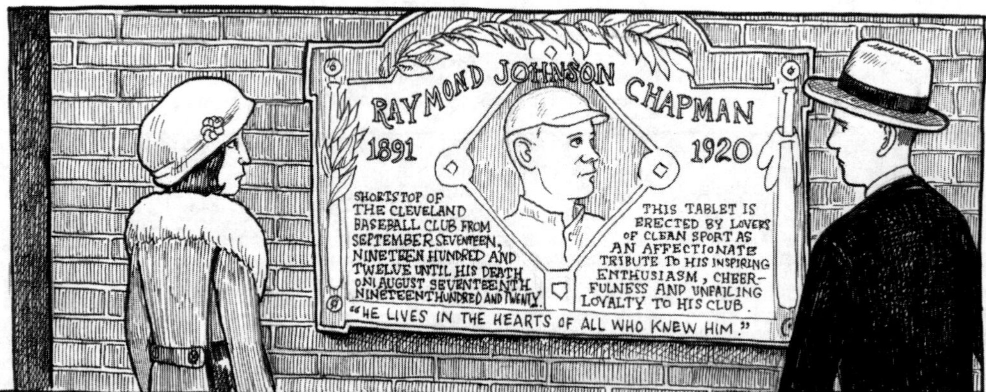

A 175-POUND BRONZE PLAQUE DEDICATED TO RAY CHAPMAN AND PAID FOR BY FAN DONATIONS WAS INSTALLED AT LEAGUE PARK'S ENTRANCE IN 1921.

IN THE 1940'S, WHEN OLD LEAGUE PARK WAS ABANDONED FOR MUNICIPAL STADIUM (AND AGAIN WHEN THE TEAM MOVED TO JACOBS FIELD), THE TABLET WAS PACKED UP... AND PROMPTLY LOST.

IT LANGUISHED IN STORAGE UNTIL 2007 WHEN IT WAS RECOVERED PURELY BY ACCIDENT, FILTHY AND FORGOTTEN.

THE PLAQUE HAS SINCE BEEN FULLY RESTORED, INSTALLED IN A PLACE OF HONOR AT THE CLEVELAND INDIANS HALL OF FAME AT THE CLUB'S CURRENT PARK, PROGRESSIVE FIELD.

CARL MAYS HAD HIS BEST YEAR YET IN 1921, BUT AMID RUMORS THAT HE HAD A HAND IN THROWING THE '21 WORLD SERIES, ALONG WITH DECLINING RELATIONS WITH MANAGER HUGGINS...

... THE YANKEES SOLD HIM TO CINCINNATI PRIOR TO THE 1924 SEASON.

HE REMAINED WITH THEM FOR FIVE SEASONS, AND ENDED HIS CAREER WITH THE GIANTS IN 1929.

WITH HIS PLAYING DAYS OVER, THE MAYS FAMILY MOVED TO OREGON. SHORTLY THEREAFTER HE LOST ALMOST EVERYTHING IN THE STOCK MARKET CRASH, AND HAD TO GO BACK TO PITCHING IN THE MINORS FOR A FEW YEARS FOR THE MONEY.

ISN'T THAT CARL MAYS?
WELL, I'LL BE...

THEN, A CRUSHING BLOW: CARL'S WIFE, FREDDIE, DIED SUDDENLY IN 1934. SHE WAS JUST THIRTY-SIX.

MAYS SOON REMARRIED, AND HE AND HIS SECOND WIFE RAISED HIS TWO CHILDREN TOGETHER. HE SCOUTED FOR VARIOUS BALL CLUBS, HUNTED, FISHED-- AND EVENTUALLY FOUND GREAT FULFILLMENT RUNNING THE OREGON BASEBALL SCHOOL FOR BOYS. HE WAS WELL-LIKED BY BOTH THE COMMUNITY AND THE PROMISING YOUNG ATHLETES WHOSE TALENT HE HELPED FOSTER.

OVERALL, HIS POST-PLAYING YEARS WERE LIVED OUT IN RELATIVE COMFORT AND CONTENTMENT.

DID BASEBALL LEARN ANYTHING FROM THE BEANING THAT LED TO CHAPMAN'S DEATH? DID HE AND MAYS LEAVE ANY LASTING MARK ON THE GAME AND THE WAY IT IS PLAYED? NOWADAYS WHEN THESE TWO COME UP, IT IS ALMOST ALWAYS IN TANDEM, A MACABRE FOOTNOTE, CHARACTERS IN A GHOULISH AND MOSTLY-FORGOTTEN STORY FROM THE GAME'S VERY DISTANT PAST.

DID YOU KNOW THAT ONCE A GUY WAS BEANED, AND THEN, LIKE... DIED?
NO WAY! WHO?
UH... I FORGET. WANT ANOTHER BEER?

MOST OF WHAT PEOPLE KNOW -- IF INDEED THEY KNOW ANYTHING -- ABOUT CARL MAYS, RAY CHAPMAN, AND THE EFFECT THAT THIS INCIDENT HAD ON BASEBALL IS, IN FACT, TOTALLY WRONG.

BALLPLAYERS STARTED WEARING HELMETS AFTER THIS HAPPENED, RIGHT? SO THIS TERRIBLE EVENT BROUGHT IMPORTANT SAFETY ISSUES TO LIGHT... AND HE DIDN'T DIE IN VAIN.

WELL... NOT EXACTLY. GUESS WHAT YEAR HELMETS BECAME MANDATORY IN THE MAJOR LEAGUES?

NOPE... LATER. MUCH LATER.

SORRY.

UM... NO.

1971. AND EVEN THEN THERE WERE PLAYERS WHO'D BEEN GRANDFATHERED IN AND DIDN'T HAVE TO COMPLY.

BOB MONTGOMERY, THE FINAL HELMET HOLDOUT

THE FIRST TEAM TO START USING HEAD PROTECTION WAS THE 1941 DODGERS, AFTER THEIR GENERAL MANAGER SAW TWO OF HIS PLAYERS SUFFER SEVERE BEANINGS...

Dodgers
Dodgers
ARE YOU SERIOUS?
HEY-A GUY DIED ONCE.

BY THE 1960'S, HELMETS (OR PROTECTIVE CAP LINERS, AT LEAST) WERE IN WIDE USE. BUT IT WASN'T UNTIL THAT 1971 SEASON-- A FULL HALF-CENTURY AFTER CHAPMAN'S DEATH-- THAT THEY WERE ABSOLUTELY REQUIRED.

The SPITBALL.

THEY OUTLAWED THE SPITBALL BECAUSE OF THE CHAPMAN INCIDENT.
Y'KNOW, 'CAUSE THE PITCH THAT KILLED HIM WAS A SPITBALL.

ACTUALLY, TEAM OWNERS HAD STARTED THE (SLOW) PROCESS OF PHASING OUT THE SPITBALL BY THE START OF BASEBALL'S 1920 SEASON.

THE START OF THE 1920 SEASON? BUT THAT MEANS...

YEAH. IT HAD NOTHING TO DO WITH THE FATAL BEANING.

IT WAS DECREED AT THE 1919 WINTER MEETINGS THAT EACH TEAM COULD SPECIFY TWO PITCHERS WHO COULD CONTINUE TO USE THE SPITBALL LEGALLY. IN TWO YEARS THAT NUMBER WOULD BE HALVED.

* NO ONE EVER CALLED THEM THAT. HOPEFULLY.

AND WHILE THE RUMOR PERSISTS THAT IT WAS A SPITBALL THAT HIT RAY CHAPMAN ON THAT AUGUST AFTERNOON IN 1920, THAT'S NOT TRUE, EITHER. WHILE MAYS WAS CONSIDERED SOMETHING OF A "FREAK PITCHER"...

...THAT WAS DUE TO HIS STRANGE PITCHING DELIVERY, NOT BALL-TAMPERING.

CHAPMAN WAS HIT BY A FASTBALL. OR A CURVEBALL, DEPENDING ON WHO YOU ASK. BUT IT WASN'T A SPITTER.

OKAY... THERE WAS ONE MODIFICATION TO THE GAME. AND IT WAS A BIG ONE. IN FACT, IT TURNED OUT TO BE THE DEATH KNELL OF A LITTLE THING KNOWN AS THE DEADBALL ERA.

HUH? THEY SWITCHED TO THE LIVELY BALL? BUT... THAT DOESN'T MAKE ANY SENSE!

NO, THE BALL ITSELF DIDN'T CHANGE. BUT IN 1920, TEAM OWNERS—LOOKING TO CUT CORNERS AND SAVE CASH—HAD BEGUN PRESSURING UMPIRES TO KEEP EACH BALL IN PLAY FOR AS LONG AS POSSIBLE. THE RESULT? BASEBALLS THAT WERE COVERED IN FILTH AND SCRATCHES, HARDER TO SEE AND TRACK THAN EVER.

ALL OF THE WITNESSES TO CHAPPIE'S BEANING AGREED THAT HE MADE NO ATTEMPT TO GET OUT OF THE WAY. IN ALL LIKELIHOOD, HE NEVER SAW THAT BASEBALL ROCKETING TOWARDS HIS TEMPLE.

SO THE UMPIRES WERE PERMITTED TO INTRODUCE FRESH BALLS MORE OFTEN. AND A BALL LESS SODDEN WITH MUD, SPIT, AND TOBACCO JUICE WAS EASIER TO SEE, MORE AERODYNAMICALLY PREDICTABLE, AND SIMPLY EASIER TO HIT... FURTHER.

HO-HUM
CRUD. I THINK I MAY HAVE TO START PLAYING DEEPER...
FLY BALL!
1919
1921

THERE WAS NO "LIVELY BALL" (STUDIES HAVE SHOWN THAT THE BALL ITSELF WAS EXACTLY THE SAME) BUT BETWEEN THE PROLIFERATION OF CLEAN BALLS AND THE GROWING RESTRICTIONS ON THE SPITBALL—NOT TO MENTION AN INCREASING INTEREST IN THE SLUGGING STYLE POPULARIZED BY BABE RUTH—THE BATTING EXPLOSION OF THE 1920'S WAS UNDERWAY.

THE HALL-OF-FAME QUESTION

NEITHER OF THESE MEN IS A MEMBER OF BASEBALL'S HALL OF FAME.*

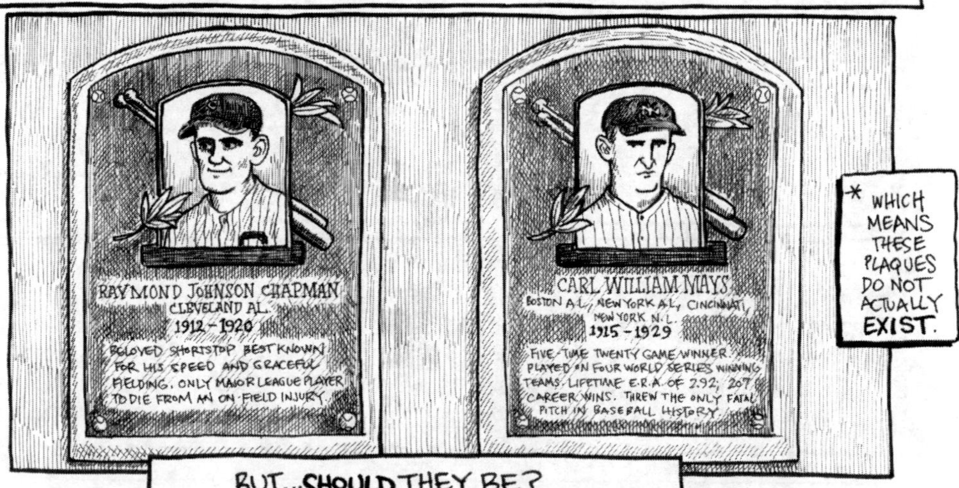

RAYMOND JOHNSON CHAPMAN
CLEVELAND A.L.
1912 – 1920
BELOVED SHORTSTOP BEST KNOWN FOR HIS SPEED AND GRACEFUL FIELDING. ONLY MAJOR LEAGUE PLAYER TO DIE FROM AN ON-FIELD INJURY.
CARL WILLIAM MAYS
BOSTON A.L., NEW YORK A.L., CINCINNATI, NEW YORK N.L.
1915 – 1929
FIVE-TIME TWENTY GAME WINNER. PLAYED ON FOUR WORLD SERIES WINNING TEAMS. LIFETIME E.R.A. OF 2.92; 207 CAREER WINS. THREW THE ONLY FATAL PITCH IN BASEBALL HISTORY.
*WHICH MEANS THESE PLAQUES DO NOT ACTUALLY **EXIST**.

BUT...**SHOULD** THEY BE? DOES EITHER OF THEM **BELONG**?

FIRST, **RAY CHAPMAN**. THE MOST IMMEDIATE ROADBLOCK TO HIS INCLUSION IS THE LENGTH OF HIS CAREER: HE PLAYED JUST NINE SEASONS, AND THE MINIMUM IS TEN, RENDERING HIM INELIGIBLE. THE ONLY WAIVER OF THIS RULE IN HALL OF FAME HISTORY WAS FOR ANOTHER CLEVELAND PLAYER WHO MET AN UNTIMELY END...

...ADDIE JOSS, WHO DIED SUDDENLY OF MENINGITIS IN 1911.

BY ALL ACCOUNTS, JOSS WAS AN ABSOLUTELY **PHENOMENAL** PLAYER. HIS LIFETIME 1.89 E.R.A. IS STILL SECOND-LOWEST OF ALL TIME. NOW, THERE'S NO QUESTION THAT CHAPPIE WAS A VALUABLE PLAYER BUT DIDN'T SHINE NEARLY AS BRIGHTLY AS JOSS DID DURING HIS EQUALLY BRIEF CAREER. HIS .278 CAREER BATTING AVERAGE MAY SEEM A BIT LIGHT, BUT HE WAS THE BEST-HITTING SHORTSTOP OF HIS CONTEMPORARIES, AND HIS SPEED WAS DEFINITELY UNRIVALED.

CHAPPIE CERTAINLY **COULD** HAVE HAD A HALL OF FAME-CALIBER CAREER, AND INDEED MANY SUSPECT HE WOULD HAVE...

HE SIMPLY **NEVER GOT THE CHANCE**.

AS HE GREW OLDER AND WATCHED A NUMBER OF HIS FORMER TEAMMATES AND COMPETITORS FETED BY THE HALL OF FAME—MANY, IN HIS ESTIMATION, LESSER PLAYERS THAN HIMSELF—**CARL MAYS** GREW CONVINCED HE WAS BEING UNFAIRLY EXCLUDED.

NOBODY REMEMBERS ANYTHING ABOUT ME EXCEPT ONE THING: THAT A PITCH I THREW CAUSED A MAN TO **DIE**.

AS FAR AS HE WAS CONCERNED, THE ACCIDENT IN WHICH HE PLAYED AN UNFORTUNATE PART WAS THE ONE OBSTACLE DENYING HIM ENTRY INTO THE HALL, AND OVER THE YEARS HIS BITTERNESS GREW. AS EASY AS IT WOULD BE TO ASCRIBE THIS TO MAYS' PERSONALITY—HE WAS EASILY SLIGHTED, PERHAPS HAD A BIT OF A PERSECUTION COMPLEX—HIS STATISTICS BEGIN TO MAKE THE CASE FOR HIM.

- Career Won-Loss Record: **208-126**
- Career Earned Run Average: **2.92**
- Career Winning Percentage: **.623**
- Played on **4** World Series and **2** pennant-winning teams
- Won **20** games in a season **5** times.

AS MAYS PUT IT SHORTLY BEFORE HIS DEATH IN 1971, ON THE OCCASION OF RUBE MARQUARD'S* INDUCTION TO THE HALL:
HE WAS A **GREAT PITCHER**.
BUT MY RECORD IS SO FAR SUPERIOR THAT IT MAKES ME WONDER...
I GUESS THEY JUST DON'T LIKE ME.
*201-177, 3.08 E.R.A

THAT FEW PLAYERS...OR MANAGERS...OR OWNERS...OR WRITERS WOULD ADMIT TO LIKING MAYS WAS TRUE. BUT **PERSONALLY UNPOPULAR** PLAYERS HAD FOUND THEIR WAY INTO THE HALL BEFORE...

IT WAS MORE LIKELY A CONFLATION OF REASONS. MAYS' RECORD WAS EXCELLENT... BUT NOT SO OUTSTANDING AS TO RENDER ANY OTHER FACTORS MOOT.

MEET TY COBB, EXHIBIT A.

AND UNFORTUNATELY FOR HIS HALL OF FAME BID, THERE WERE DEFINITELY OTHER FACTORS FOR VOTERS TO MULL OVER:

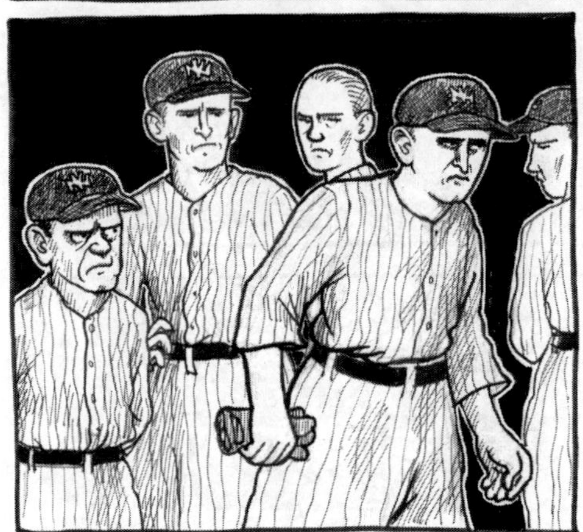

THERE WAS THE PERSISTENT RUMOR THAT HE WAS INVOLVED IN LOSING AT LEAST ONE WORLD SERIES GAME FOR MONEY.

Ban Johnson reacts to Mays' latest stunt.

THEN THERE WAS THE FACT THAT HE DESERTED THE RED SOX IN 1919, SETTING OFF A MAELSTROM IN THE AMERICAN LEAGUE.

FINALLY, YES -- HE DID, HOWEVER INADVERTENTLY, THROW A PITCH THAT KILLED A MAN. NO ONE THINKS MAYS KILLED CHAPMAN ON PURPOSE. HE WILL, HOWEVER, ALWAYS BE LINKED TO HIS DEATH, AND IT SEEMS THAT THESE QUESTIONS ABOUT HIS INTEGRITY MAKE THAT ONE GRISLY INCIDENT ALL THE **HARDER TO FORGET**.

THERE'S A BIT IN THE HALL OF FAME VOTING GUIDELINES KNOWN AS THE "**CHARACTER CLAUSE**" THAT INSTRUCTS VOTERS TO TAKE POTENTIAL INDUCTEES' "**INTEGRITY, SPORTSMANSHIP, AND CHARACTER**", AS WELL AS THEIR STATS, INTO CONSIDERATION. IT'S CONTROVERSIAL FOR MANY REASONS, ESPECIALLY NOW THAT SO MANY PLAYERS ARE SUSPECTED OF USING PERFORMANCE-ENHANCING DRUGS WITHOUT ANY PROOF WITHSTANDING. IT'S ALSO WHY SHOELESS JOE JACKSON, PETE ROSE, AND PLAYERS NAMED IN RECENT DOPING SCANDALS WILL PROBABLY NEVER GAIN ENTRY TO THE HALL.

COOPERSTOWN
YOU MUST BE THIS MORALLY UPSTANDING TO ENTER.

PERCEIVED CHEATING OF ANY KIND IS THE ANTITHESIS OF THAT WOBBLY TERM, "SPORTSMANSHIP."

LOOKING AT THE NUMBERS MAYS POSTED OVER HIS CAREER, ONE MIGHT THINK HE WAS ALREADY A HALL OF FAMER. IT WOULDN'T BE SURPRISING TO FIND A PLAYER OF HIS CALIBER THERE. SEVERAL MEN POSSESSING (ARGUABLY) LESSER CREDENTIALS RESIDE WITH THE ALL-TIME GREATS.

HUH. YOU KNOW THAT GUY WHO KILLED THE OTHER GUY IN THAT BEANING?
YEAH?
HE WAS ACTUALLY... WOW. HE WAS **PRETTY DAMN GOOD.**

CARL MAYS?
OFFICIAL VETERANS COMMITTEE BALLOT 2009
HA! DREAM ON!

HE HAS APPEARED ON THE BALLOT REPEATEDLY, MOST RECENTLY IN 2009. HE NEEDED NINE VOTES; HE GOT LESS THAN THREE (THE LOWEST VOTE-GETTERS' TOTALS WERE NOT RELEASED).

CARL MAYS COULD BE IN THE HALL OF FAME BUT TO GET INDUCTED, YOU NEED TO BE **ELECTED**.

AND THAT WILL **NEVER HAPPEN**.

RAYMOND JOHNSON CHAPMAN
1891
1920
Indians
Carl Mays, Yankee Whose Pitch Killed Batter in 1920, Is Dead
SAN DIEGO, April 5 (AP)—
Carl Mays, the New York
Yankees pitcher who threw
the fastball that hit and killed
Cleveland batter Ray Chapman
n 1920, died yesterday in El
on Valley Hospital. He was
years old.
ys, who won 208 games as
hurler for four major league
s, was later a scout for
years.
right-hander, whose spec-
was the submarine pitch,
ff the effects of Chapman's
eath to finish the 1920
with 26 victories. He
fastly maintained that
an, a right-handed hit-
tstop, lunged out of
er's box in the game
lo Grounds in which
hit.
following year Mays
27-9 record for the
his career high.
he was traded to the
Reds and posted
9 losses. He was
the Reds in 1926.
ened run average
him 14th among
he pitched
n Yankee Sta-
April 18, 1923
a roommate of Babe
Ruth. He finished his playing career with the New York
Giants but remained in baseball
as a scout for Milwaukee and Cleveland.
Carl Mays as a Yankee
Surviving are his widow,
Esther, a son, Carl Junior, and
a daughter, Mrs. Betty Barker.

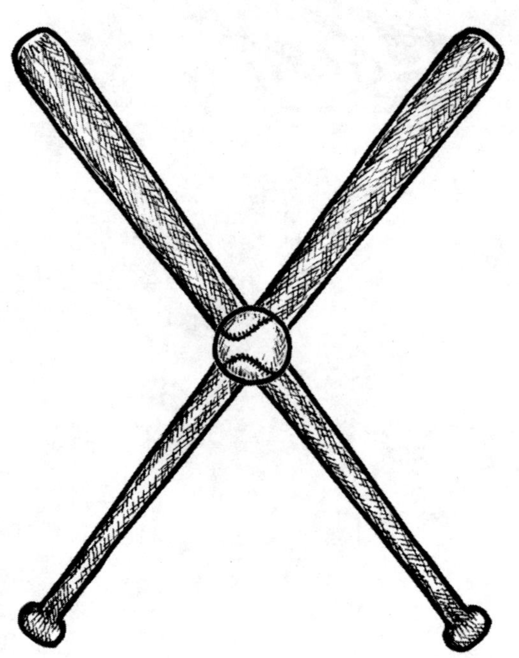

Bibliography

The Cleveland Plain Dealer (newspaper) August 17–19, October 4, 1920.

Curran, William. *Big Sticks: The Batting Revolution of the Twenties*. New York: William Morrow and Company, Inc., 1990.

Epting, Chris. *The Early Polo Grounds: Images of Baseball.* Charleston, SC: Arcadia Publishing, 2009.

Gay, Timothy. *Tris Speaker: The Rough and Tumble Life of a Baseball Legend.* Connecticut: Morris Book Publishing, 2007.

James, Bill. *The Bill James Historical Baseball Abstract.* New York: Villard Books, 1988.

Jones, David. D. *Deadball Stars of the American League.* Dulles, Va.: Potomac Books, Inc., 2006.

Lieb, Fred. *Baseball As I Have Known It.* New York: Coward, McCann & Geoghegan, Inc., 1977.

McGarigle, Bob. *Baseball's Great Tragedy: The Story of Carl Mays, Submarine Pitcher.* New York: Exposition Press, 1972.

Ritter, Lawrence S. *The Glory of Their Times: The Story of the Early Days of Baseball Told by the Men Who Played It*. New York: Perennial/Harper Collins, 2002

Simon, Tom. *Deadball Stars of the National League.* Washington, D. C.: Brassey's, 2004.

Sowell, Mike. *The Pitch That Killed: The Story of Carl Mays, Ray Chapman, and the Pennant Race of 1920.* Chicago: Ivan R. Dee, 1989.

Swirsky, Seth. *Every Pitcher Tells a Story: Letters Gathered by a Devoted Baseball Fan*. New York: Times Books/Random House, 1999.

McFarland Graphic Novels

Yellow Rose of Texas: The Myth of Emily Morgan.
Written by Douglas Brode; Illustrated by Joe Orsak. 2010

Horrors: Great Stories of Fear and Their Creators.
Written by Rocky Wood; Illustrated by Glenn Chadbourne. 2010

Hutch: Baseball's Fred Hutchinson and a Legacy of Courage.
Written by Mike Shannon; Illustrated by Scott Hannig. 2011

Hit by Pitch: Ray Chapman, Carl Mays and the Fatal Fastball. Molly Lawless. 2012

Werewolves of Wisconsin and Other American Myths, Monsters and Ghosts. Andy Fish. 2012

Witch Hunts: A Graphic History of the Burning Times.
Written by Rocky Wood and Lisa Morton;
Illustrated by Greg Chapman. 2012

Virgin Vampires: Or, Once Upon a Time in Transylvania.
Written by Douglas Brode; Illustrated by Joe Orsak. 2012